HIS LAST COMMAND
OUR FIRST PRIORITY

HIS LAST COMMAND

OUR FIRST PRIORITY

JACK HANES

Copyright © 2002 Megalife Ministries
Reprinted 2004
PO Box 737
Kingswood, N.S.W. 2747 Australia
Email: pen.clc.mi@pnc.com.au
www.worldchangersnetwork.com.au

Published by Megalife Ministries
PO Box 737
Kingswood, N.S.W. 2747 Australia
Email: pen.clc.mi@pnc.com.au
www.worldchangersnetwork.com.au

All rights reserved. No part of this book may be reproduced, stored in a retrieval system, or transmitted in any form or by any means electronic, mechanical, photocopy, recording or otherwise without the prior permission of the publisher, except for brief quotations in printed reviews or articles.

Unless otherwise indicated, all Scripture quotations are taken from the *New King James Version*. Copyright © 1979, 1980, 1982 by Thomas Nelson, Inc. Used by permission. All rights reserved.

Scripture quotations marked (NIV) are taken from the *Holy Bible, New International Version*®.NIV® Copyright © 1973, 1978, 1984 by International Bible Society. Used by permission of Zondervan Publishing House. All rights reserved.

Scripture quotations marked (TLB) are taken from *The Living Bible* © 1971. Used by permission of Tyndale House Publishers, Inc.,Wheaton, Illinois 60189. All rights reserved.

Scripture quotations marked (The Message) are taken from *THE MESSAGE*. Copyright © 1993,1994,1995,1996,2000,2001,2002. Used by permission of NavPress Publishing Group.

Scripture quotations marked (GNB) are taken from the *Good News Translation* revised edition © American Bible Society. Used by permission of Bible Society in Australia.

Scripture quotations marked (KJV) are taken from the *King James Version* of the Bible.

Scripture quotations on the inside front cover and back cover are taken from the *Holy Bible,* New Living Translation, copyright © 1996. Used by permission of Tyndale House Publishers, Inc., Wheaton, Illinois 60189. All rights reserved.

American spelling has been used throughout this book.

National Library of Australia
Cataloguing-in-Publication Data:

Hanes, Jack, 1952 -
His last command : our first priority.

ISBN 0 9750052 0 0.

1. Missions. 2. Evangelistic work. I. Megalife Ministries.
II. Title.

266.023

Cover designed by Allleen Lowe
Quote on front cover by Robert Moffat
Printed by Griffin Press

"Go and make disciples of all nations"

Matthew 28:19

DEDICATION

This book is dedicated to the 35,000 people who died today, who lived their entire life on this planet and never once heard the name of Jesus.

ACKNOWLEDGEMENTS

I want to acknowledge the best wife a man could ever hope for. Carol is my hero. How I honor and admire her as a person, as a Christian, as a mother, and as a minister of the Lord Jesus Christ.

Carol and I both want to thank our incredible secretary and personal assistant, Karina Day. Without her tireless effort this book simply would not have happened. To be honest with you most of my ministry wouldn't happen if it weren't for her. Karina, you are a legend. We can't thank you enough.

Thanks Amelia for hours of typing, cutting, pasting, editing and giving your best.

Thanks to Rob De Martin our business manager. Rob, I owe so much to you. Thank you with all my heart.

Someone has said that nobody ever has any true success unless a lot of other people want him or her to. If there is success in my life then it is because of a lot of other people.

Thanks, Ric, Matt, James, Barry, Reg, Mick, Ian. Thanks Ps. Messer, Ps. Gibbs, Kevin, and

Ralph. Thanks Lorna for praying. Thanks Stevie, Carissa and Jojo, I love you. Thanks team and staff of Penrith Christian Life Centre. Thanks Tim and Graham.

Thank you Lord for all these wonderful people who have enriched my life.

Jack Hanes

CONTENTS

Foreword 13

Introduction 17

Preface 19

Chapter 1: If I Were The Devil 23

Chapter 2: The Master Key To Abundant Living 51

Chapter 3: Driving Out The Money Changers 67

Chapter 4: Knowing Why You Have What You Have 87

Chapter 5: Will God's Will Be Done? 101

Chapter 6: The Compassion To Deliver Nations 125

Chapter 7: The Father's Heart 139

Chapter 8: Let's Go To The Other Side 159

Chapter 9: That None Should Perish 175

Chapter 10: God's Plan For the Ages 199

FOREWORD

A million lost people enter eternity every week, but God has a way to reverse that heartbreaking statistic…a strategy that includes us!

Jack Hanes has stirred me…my family…and our church to increase our passion for souls - and he will stir you up, too. This book is so compelling it should be labeled with a warning: **"BEWARE: Do not read this book if you are a *contented* Christian."** It will stun you, shake you, and light a fire within you for spiritual greatness.

Through Scripture, Jack explains that the devil knows his days are numbered, but you and I can determine how much time he actually has left. Because of that, the *devil's #1 priority* is…to stop you from fulfilling your mission. You will discover the devil's strategies to keep his position and take away your power…and there is so much more.

God is recruiting an army of people who will take His Word to the world - people who will make Jesus' "last command" *their* "first priority." The book you hold in your hands is one of God's *most* powerful recruiting manuals.

What will you do with it?

Dr Marilyn Hickey

Jack Hanes is a "man after God's own heart." His love and passion for souls is infectious and the purity of his life, marriage, and ministry is exemplary. I am honored to know he and Carol and have developed a deep, meaningful relationship to reach the nations. Jack and I are involved together in the "Principle of Twelve" as Jesus developed it, to mobilize leaders for the final harvest. His impact in Australia and the entire Pacific Rim is being multiplied through this powerful principle!

Our church at Bethany World Prayer Center has been powerfully impacted as a "First Priority" church. Missions has always been strong for us with a commitment to give 25 per cent of our income to local and foreign missions. However, Jack's ministry to us moved us to the next level. We now have a monthly "Missions Sunday" and our members are heavily involved in the planting of 500 churches this year. It all came through the passionate message he preached on "Others." *(The Master Key To Abundant Living - see Chapter 2).*

Those who can communicate God's heart for world missions are few and far between. The book you are holding is one of those rare insights into a world vision and "without a vision the people PERISH." God will prosper every church which possesses at its core a vision for the world. When you combine a "vision" ("First Priority") with a "principle" ("the Principle of Twelve"), you have WORLD IMPACT.

Read this, follow it, implement it, and watch God awaken your church to the march of the Holy Spirit's drumbeat: "His Last Command, Our First Priority."

Ps Larry Stockstill

INTRODUCTION

I had just flown back to Australia from Singapore and was picked up from the airport by two businessmen who were taking me to my next meeting. As I rode in their late model German made car one of them asked me, "So tell us Jack, where is it really tough right now out there on the mission field?"

I had just spent the past weekend doing a mission's conference and then the next three days were spent with the missionaries and staff at a retreat in nearby Malaysia. So I began to tell them of some of the lives of the missionaries I had just met. There was the brother from Nepal who has suffered persecution for preaching the Gospel. There were the two brothers from Pakistan who live in danger every day. And there was the brother from Sri Lanka whose close friend was killed for preaching the love of Christ, his body riddled with 60 bullets. As I shared these stories with them I told them that the need in the world was great. I told them of the 35,000 people who died every day having never heard the name of Jesus one time in their entire life. Just then the business man in the back seat, in an attitude that sounded smug and maybe even cynical asked, "So what do you think happens to all those people?" I paused a moment and said, "Well, the Bible says that there is no other name for people to be saved except the name of Jesus. But that's not the question that bothers me nearly as much as what's going to happen to the people who had the Gospel and were commanded to get it to all those perishing people but never did. What's going to happen to them? They were entrusted with the good news. They were commissioned and empowered by the Holy Spirit. They were responsible for delivering it, but didn't. What's going to happen to them?"

It got quiet in that car.

Before we reached the conference where I was going to preach, those two businessmen were strategizing how they could plant churches in China through their business.

PREFACE

In 1986 I was sitting in a restaurant in Yuma Arizona (USA) with my pastor, Tom Messer. We were enjoying a wonderful meal after a great Sunday night service. I had just returned from the most exciting month of my life in the Kalahari Desert and the Okavango swamps of Botswana.

For 11 years I had been the associate pastor of Mt. Zion Church. As we ate, Pastor Messer began sharing with me a vision that his wife, Noel, had whilst I was in Africa. She saw a map of Australia and over the map babies started falling out of the sky. People were on the ground with baskets, trying to catch the babies. But the babies were falling faster than people could catch them. God said, "Get your basket down to Australia and get ready for what I'm going to do in that land."

At the end of that story, Pastor Messer asked me if Carol and I would be willing to go to Australia and pioneer our first overseas church. We had just bought a beautiful new home with a fireplace, swimming pool and grand piano.

We had been in it less than five months. I said, "Pastor, if you want us to do this we will go. You're my pastor, I love you and I believe God leads me through godly leadership."

I had no burden for Australia, no calling, no knowledge of its culture or spiritual condition. I didn't even know if they spoke English. I found out later that they don't (just kidding…they sort of speak English!)

With my faithful and courageous wife and three small children we sold everything, packed 11 duffel bags with clothes and on August 24 1987 we landed in Sydney.

We didn't have a clue. How do you start a church in a nation where only about 2 per cent of the population attends church? We started from scratch. Carol and I began knocking on doors. I would put the baby in a backpack and go down one side of the street and Carol would have the two little children going down the other side of the street. It took us three years to get 50 people to come to our church. We would work up to one hundred hours in a week. Getting up at 4:00am or 5:00am for two to three hours of prayer and then out delivering brochures all day and sometimes into the night.

The first Sunday that we had enough people to have a church service we took up our first missionary offering. We declared that we were a Missions Church and that Jesus' last command to go into all the world and preach the Gospel was our *first priority*. A few months later we had our first Missions Conference and asked the people to fill out a faith promise card for missions. The first year we faith promised $6,000.00 dollars and started planting churches in Indonesia.

We have had a Missions Conference every year since then and are now able to release over a million dollars a year to missions, planting hundreds of churches a year around the world. The last six years have seen us plant 1322 churches throughout India, China, Indonesia and other great nations of the world. We are believing the Lord that what we now give in a year, which is now approximately 50 per cent of our church's income, we will give in a month.

I believe the Great Commission is what justifies the Church's existence on the earth.

Everything we do on a Sunday in our church services we really don't need to be on the earth to do. We could do everything we do here, in heaven: praise, teach, fellowship, share, give, take communion. The only thing we can do here that we can't do in heaven is get the Gospel to perishing people. We won't be able to do that there.

And that is the one thing Jesus has commanded us to do. This is His Great Commission to us. This is why we are here. It is the default call on every Christian.

He said, "Go into all the world and preach the Gospel." It was His last command. It must become our *first priority*.

CHAPTER ONE
IF I WERE THE DEVIL

If I Were The Devil

The Bible has a lot to say about the devil. He's been around for a long time; deceiving, murdering, working catastrophic chaos and mindless, merciless mayhem in the earth.

John 8:44
"You belong to your father, the devil, and you want to carry out your father's desire. He was a murderer from the beginning, not holding to the truth, for there is no truth in him. When he lies, he speaks his native language, for he is a liar and the father of lies." (NIV)

Revelation 12:9
"So the great dragon was cast out, that serpent of old, called the Devil and Satan, who deceives the whole world; he was cast to the earth, and his angels were cast out with him."

If I were the devil I would know from my time in heaven, and my past experiences with God, that God's Word always comes to pass. God always speaks the truth, and He never lies. I would hate it. I would not want people to know it. But in my shriveled up little heart

I would know it's true.

Numbers 23:19
"God is not a man, that He should lie, nor a son of man, that He should repent; has He said, and will He not do it? Or has He spoken, and will He not make it good?"

Titus 1:2
"...in hope of eternal life which God, who cannot lie, promised before time began."

If I were the devil I'd know that God cannot lie and I would also know everything He'd said about me and about my future.

Revelation 20:10
"The devil, who deceived them, was cast into the lake of fire and brimstone where the beast and the false prophet are. And they will be tormented day and night forever and ever."

If I were the devil I'd know that that is exactly what is going to happen to me and there is absolutely nothing I can do about it.

> *God's Word makes it very clear not only what is going to happen to the devil, but when it's going to happen.*

God's Word makes it very clear not only what is going to happen to the devil, but when it's going to happen.

Mark 13:10
"And the Gospel must first be preached to all the nations."

Matthew 24:14
"And this Gospel of the kingdom will be preached in all the world as a witness to all the nations, and then the end will come."

If I were the devil I would know that before the inevitable happened to me, the Gospel has to first be preached to all nations. As long as the Gospel is kept from being preached to all the nations, I'm okay, I'm cool; I'm still in the earth and not in hell. I'm still running around with my little Marilyn Manson groupies and my little dark entourage. I'm still here.

If I were the devil my first priority

OUR FIRST PRIORITY

would be to see to it that the Gospel is not preached to the world. All my power, my whole kingdom, all of my demonic resources would be totally committed to stopping the Gospel from spreading. *My whole survival would depend on it!*

The Bible teaches us an amazing truth in the second letter of Peter. Look at this verse with me.

2 Peter 3:11-12
"Therefore, since all these things will be dissolved, what manner of persons ought you to be in holy conduct and godliness, looking for and hastening the coming of the day of God, because of which the heavens will be dissolved, being on fire, and the elements will melt with fervent heat?"

> *Jesus has always meant for His delay in returning to this earth to be a short one.*

Jesus has always meant for His delay in returning to this earth to be a short one.

The Living Bible says it this way, "You should look forward to that day and hurry it along - the day when God will set the heavens on fire, and the heavenly bodies will melt and disappear in flames." (2 Peter 3:11-12)

I am not only to look forward to that great day but I am to hurry it up. The Bible says, "looking for AND hastening that day."

Jesus never intended a long delay in His return to the earth.

Revelation 3:11
"Behold, I am coming quickly! Hold fast what you have, that no one may take your crown."

Revelation 22:7
"Behold, I am coming quickly! Blessed is he who keeps the words of the prophecy of this book."

Revelation 22:12
"And behold, I am coming quickly, and My reward is with Me, to give to every one according to his work."

OUR FIRST PRIORITY

Revelation 22:20
"He who testifies to these things says, 'Surely I am coming quickly.' Amen. Even so, come, Lord Jesus!'"

His purpose has always been to return soon. He says we are to hasten His return, we are to hurry it along, we are to speed it up and make it happen. He is anxious to return. And while we wait for His return, He waits for us to go forth.

We say, "Come sweet Lord." And He says, "Go sweet Church."

"Come Lord!"

"Go Church!"

> *He's not coming till we get going.*

We're praying, "Come." He's commanding, "Go."

And the truth is He isn't coming till we get going.

Mark 16:15
"And He said to them, 'Go into all the world and preach the Gospel to every creature.'"

Matthew 24:14
"And this Gospel of the kingdom will be

preached in all the world, as a witness to all the nations; and then the end will come."

We must go so He can come. Our focus has been the coming of the Lord – His focus has been the going of the Church. I'll bet there are whole schools of angels in heaven arguing over the doctrine of when the Church will go.

If I were the devil I would be totally committed to keeping the Church from going into all the world and preaching the Gospel to every creature so that the end would not come! If I were the devil I would see Christians who were totally committed to Jesus' last command as my greatest threat and worst nightmare. If I were the devil I would have schemes and strategies to keep the Gospel from getting to people. And I would work at it like my eternal destiny depended on it!

2 Corinthians 4:4
"The god of this age has blinded the minds of unbelievers, so that they cannot see the light of the gospel of the glory of Christ, who is the

OUR FIRST PRIORITY

image of God." (NIV)

Satan is not only trying to damn mankind - he's trying to preserve himself!

2 Corinthians 11:3
"But I fear, lest somehow, as the serpent deceived Eve by his craftiness, so your minds may be corrupted from the simplicity that is in Christ."

> *Satan is not only trying to damn mankind – he's trying to preserve himself!*

Ephesians 6:11
"Put on all of God's armor so that you will be able to stand safe against all strategies and tricks of Satan." (TLB)

2 Corinthians 2:11
"…in order that Satan might not outwit us. For we are not unaware of his schemes." (NIV)

You better believe I'd have plans and schemes and strategies. I'd tell every despicable,

If I Were The Devil

damnable, bald, bold face lie I could tell. I would deceive, disguise and disgust! I would use despair and despondency to dishearten and discourage anybody who took seriously Jesus' command to go save the world.

I would mock and jeer
Intimidate and cause fear
Ridicule and sneer
And sadistically leer
I would stop up the ear
And confuse what they hear
I would provoke them to veer
Without mercy or tear
Keep the Gospel unclear
Make the price seem too dear
Their souls I will shear
To keep Him from drawing near
And my future right here.

Let me tell you what I would do if I were the devil. I would have at least six, yes that is a good devil number, six strategies to keep the Church from making Jesus' last command their *first priority.*

OUR FIRST PRIORITY

First:

I would marginalize missions. I would departmentalize missions. I would take it off the main page and put it in the margin somewhere. I would put it on the very busy list of all the other very busy things of church life. I would make it a department in the church and put it somewhere near the 'ladies quilting fellowship'. I would do all I could to keep it from becoming the *first priority* of the local church.

I would see to it that pastors had a missions PROGRAM, and not a missions PASSION. I would make sure the church had a missions DEPARTMENT, not a missions DYNAMIC. I would ensure Christians had a missions CONSCIENCE, but not a missions COMMITMENT.

Yes, I would definitely marginalize missions.

There was a time in our early Church history where for almost 300 years not one missionary was sent out. Not one. The *first priority* of the Church was keeping her doctrine pure. And while she focused on her 'pure' doctrine, generations of people perished without the

Gospel.

If I were the devil I would keep the Church so busy with all its departments and so anxious about the hundreds of details that are involved in running a church that they wouldn't have the time or resources for missions.

> *If I were the devil I would see that the main thing is to keep the main thing from becoming the main thing.*

If I were the devil I would get senior pastors to focus on their finances, their facilities, and their frequent flyer points, not the doomed, the damned, and the dying. I would see to it that they focused on everything but the main thing. If I were the devil I would see that the main thing is to keep the main thing from becoming the main thing.

The Apostle Paul said, "This one thing I do…" (Philippians 3:13)

I would have that interpreted as, "These 100 things I do…"

Sir Heneage Ogilvie
"The really idle man gets nowhere but the

perpetually busy man does not get much further."

So the first thing I would do if I were the devil would be to marginalize missions.

Second:
If I were the devil I would get Christians to focus on this world, not the next one. "Live for the temporal not the eternal. Work your whole life for a few short years of retirement. Live for right now, because right now is all you have. Don't think about eternity. Don't think about your accountability to God. Don't think that you're going to have to stand before God some day and give an answer to Him for how you lived your life and spent your money and used your time."

Someone asked Daniel Webster what was the greatest thought he ever thought. He answered, *"My greatest thought is my accountability to God."*

2 Corinthians 4:18
"So we fix our eyes not on what is seen, but on

what is unseen. For what is seen is temporary, but what is unseen is eternal." (NIV)

Romans 14:12
"So then each of us shall give account of himself to God."

If I were the devil I would see to it that Christians didn't think past lunch let alone contemplate eternity. I would do all I could to keep them focused on this little sand bar of time between the two great oceans of eternity.

> *This isn't the game. This is the tryouts for the game.*

Oh, how we've been seduced by our few moments of mortality! We live our whole lives thinking that this, right here and right now, is it. Friend, this isn't it. This isn't the game. This is just the tryouts for the game. The game is just a few heartbeats away.

Third:
If I were the devil I would teach that the purpose of prosperity is to see how many toys I

OUR FIRST PRIORITY

could buy and how many things I could accumulate before I die.

SHOP TILL YOU DROP.
BUY TILL YOU DIE.
SPEND TO THE END.

That would be my motto. I would get Christians to love earthly treasures more than heavenly treasures. I would get them to believe that temporal investment in things is more important than eternal investment in souls. I would see to it that the major focus of their money would be the accumulation of things.

Matthew 6:19-21
"Do not store up for yourselves treasures on earth, where moth and rust destroy, and where thieves break in and steal. But store up for yourselves treasures in heaven, where moth and rust do not destroy, and where thieves do not break in and steal. For where your treasure is, there your heart will be also." (NIV)

The Living Bible says it this way…

If I Were The Devil

Matthew 6:19-21
"Don't store up treasures here on earth where they can erode away or may be stolen. Store them in heaven where they will never lose their value and are safe from thieves. If your profits are in heaven, your heart will be there too."

> *"It is just as wrong to store up treasure on earth as it is to do anything else Jesus told us not to do."*

John Wesley
"It is just as wrong to store up treasure on earth, as it is to do anything else Jesus told us not to do."

Wayne Myers
"We are accountable to God for the excess and surplus in our life."

We are not owners. We are stewards. Stewards oversee someone else's goods. All that we have has been entrusted to us by God.

Roy L. Smith
"Every possession is a trust."

OUR FIRST PRIORITY

Luke 12:15

"Then he said to them, 'Watch out! Be on your guard against all kinds of greed; a man's life does not consist in the abundance of his possessions.'" (NIV)

A wealthy old man was very enthusiastic about his lovely young bride but sometimes he wondered whether she might have just married him for his money.

So he asked, "If I lost all my money, would you still love me?" She retorted, "Of course I would still love you. Don't be silly. But I would miss you!"

Fourth:

If I were the devil I would make sure that the Great Commission became the great omission. Instead of 'Go into all the world and preach the Gospel', instead of 'make disciples of all nations', I would teach a more popular doctrine – stay at home and build facilities and teach yourselves over and over again how to be His disciples.

Oswald J. Smith

"Why should anyone hear the Gospel twice before everyone has heard it once?"

If I were the devil I would convince everyone that there is plenty of time, no rush, no hurry. I would make sure that no one felt a sense of urgency for perishing people.

In my office I have an hourglass sitting on a pedestal. I am looking at it right now as I type these pages. It is about 12 inches high. The pedestal it stands on is about three feet tall. I look at it every day so that I can be reminded of the quote by Robert Moffat who said, *"We'll have all eternity to celebrate our victories, but only one short hour before sunset to win them."*

> *"We have all of eternity to celebrate our victories, but only one short hour before sunset to win them."*

Friend, all we get on this planet is about an hour. The Bible says that a 1000 years is as a day to the Lord. If that is true and if 12 hours make up the daylight part of a day, then a 70 year old man gets somewhere around

OUR FIRST PRIORITY

57 minutes.

You get an hour. You have one hour to do whatever it is you are going to do for God and then you seal forever your work for Him on this planet. The clock is ticking. I don't know if you've noticed it or not, but you're getting older. You really are. If you don't think you're getting older just go take all your clothes off and stand in front of the mirror. Gravity is working!

Your hour is almost up. The sand is racing through the hourglass. Whatever you're going to do for God you better get busy doing it.

If I were the devil I would deafen the ears of Christians to the sound of a ticking clock. Time is running out. Every man and every woman, every boy and every girl is only one heartbeat away from eternity. So are you. So am I. One heartbeat away.

1 Corinthians 7:29
"The important thing to remember is that our remaining time is very short, [and so are our opportunities for doing the Lord's work]." (TLB)

Psalm 39:4-5

"Lord, help me to realize how brief my time on earth will be. Help me to know that I am here for but a moment more. My life is no longer than my hand! My whole lifetime is but a moment to you. Proud man! Frail as breath! A shadow! And all his busy rushing ends in nothing. He heaps up riches for someone else to spend." (TLB)

Time is so short – eternity is so long. If I were the devil I'd make sure that priorities were all wrong. I'd see to it that time was wasted until an entire generation died off, leaving the task of world evangelism undone and then I would begin again with the next generation, building on the example of the last one. I would fight to make lesser priorities more important than preaching the Gospel to perishing people.

It's easy to have misguided priorities. As a matter of fact, if I were the devil I would see that

> *I would fight to make lesser priorities more important than preaching the Gospel to perishing people.*

wrong priorities would be one of my easier tasks.

Surprised to see an empty seat at the Superbowl, a diehard fan remarked about it to the woman sitting next to the empty seat. "It was my husband's," the woman explained, "But he died." "I'm very sorry," said the man. "Yet I'm really surprised that another relative, or friend, didn't jump at the chance to take the seat reserved for him." "Beats me," she said. "They all insisted on going to the funeral."

It's not hard to get people's priorities wrong.

Fifth:

If I were the devil I would encourage Christians to pray for the harvest.

By praying for the harvest Christians will think they are doing their part in the Great Commission. I would know that praying for a harvest that is already ripe is much less effective than praying for the laborers to go forth and reap the harvest.

Don't get me wrong, I believe passionately in prayer. But I believe many Christians are hiding in their prayer closets. Prayer is important beyond words. But the Bible does not teach us that prayer is the power of God unto salvation. The Gospel is. Nobody gets saved without hearing the Gospel. You and I can pray until we are blue in the face but no one will ever be converted without hearing the Gospel. Paul said in Romans that the Gospel is the power of God unto salvation. (Romans 1:16)

Jesus does not teach us to pray for the lost. He teaches us to pray for the Church…that she will go tell the lost.

John 4:35
"Do you not say, 'There are still four months and then comes the harvest'? Behold, I say to you, lift up your eyes and look at the fields, for they are already white for harvest!"

The Living Bible
"Do you think the work of harvesting will not begin until the summer ends four months from now? Look around you! Vast fields of human souls are ripening all around us, and are ready now for reaping." (John 4:35)

OUR FIRST PRIORITY

> *How effective is it to pray for a harvest that is already so ripe we are losing it faster than we can harvest it?*

How effective is it to pray for a harvest that is already so ripe we are losing it faster than we can harvest it?

Luke 10:2
"The harvest truly is great, but the laborers are few; therefore pray the Lord of the harvest to send out laborers into His harvest."

The need is for workers! Goers and givers!
The need of a ripe harvest is not for it to get any riper but for people to go and to give so that it can be harvested.

Sixth:
And finally, if I were the devil I would teach Christians that the power of the Holy Spirit has been sent to bless them.
I would see to it that there is a 'bless me' focus in the Church.

Bless me, anoint me, appoint me, prosper me, help me, heal me, deal me, fill me, thrill me, teach me, reach me, enlighten me, build me, encourage me, inspire me, satiate me, saturate me, satisfy me, appease me, please me, give me, grant me … more for me.

Please understand that I love the Holy Spirit and I am hungry for all that He has for me. I've been to Toronto, Pensacola, Tulsa, Bogotá and Korea. I love it all. I want it all. I need it all. My definition of balance is to go to all extremes equally.

But if I were the devil I would teach that the Holy Spirit has been sent to bless me in my life instead of helping me to reach the world with the Gospel.

Acts 1:8
"But you shall receive power when the Holy Spirit has come upon you; and *you shall be witnesses* to Me in Jerusalem, and in all Judea and Samaria, *and to the end of the earth*."

In the original language the Greek word for 'witness' is the word martus or martyr.

OUR FIRST PRIORITY

The reason we have been given the Holy Spirit is to give us the power to lay our life down as we are delivering the message of Christ to the ends of the earth! The Baptism of the Holy Spirit is the power to die. It is the power to give ourselves up as we proclaim His Word to the ends of the earth. The baptism of the Holy Spirit is the equipping to fulfill the Great Commission.

> *The reason we have been given the Holy Spirit is to give us the power to lay our life down as we are delivering the message of Christ to the ends of the earth!*

"When the Holy Spirit comes upon you, you will have the power to be my *martyrs* in Jerusalem and in all Judea and Samaria, *and to the end of the earth.*"(Acts 1:8)

Well, these are six things I would do if I were the devil. You and I know that he has been busy with his schemes and strategies for over 2,000 years. He's gotten away with things like marginalizing missions, distracting pastors, seducing Christians to live for the moment and love material things for two millenniums.

But something has happened in the past few decades that he has never reckoned on. A generation has risen up to embrace Jesus' last command as its *first priority*! This is his worst nightmare – his absolute worst-case scenario! Millions of Christians are not falling for his tricks any more. It is harvest time all over the world. Never before in the history of the Church have we seen global harvest like we are seeing it right now. The devil knows he has at best a few year's left!

It is harvest time all over the world. Fifty per cent of Africa has converted to Christ in the last 100 years.

Every seven weeks in Latin America a million more people are being born again. Over half of the population of Brazil and Guatemala and Honduras and El Salvador are already born again.

Forty per cent of Chile, Costa Rica, and Bolivia are Bible believing Christians.

OUR FIRST PRIORITY

> *For the first time in the history of the world the finish line is in sight.*

I had the privilege of pulling out our last Australian Assembly of God missionaries in the nation of Papua New Guinea just recently. The reason we pulled them out is because it is mission accomplished! Thirty-five per cent of that nation are born again and another thirty-five per cent are sympathetic to the cause of Christ including the government and the media.

About 35,000 Chinese a day are being born again. A million a month!

For the first time in the history of the world the finish line is in sight. It's almost done! Will you be a part of its completion? Will you buy into the greatest event in the history of the world?

If Jesus lives in your heart, you are a missionary. Going and Giving is what God has commissioned you to do.

If Jesus doesn't live in your heart you are the mission field.

CHAPTER TWO
THE MASTER KEY TO ABUNDANT LIVING

I owe a tremendous debt to Wayne Myers not only for the teaching of this chapter but for his life and example. Carol and I would not be where we are today without Wayne and Martha, two of the greatest and godliest people we have ever met.

One weekend I told my kids I was going to preach on the Master Key To Abundant Living. I told them that this master key could be described with just one word. My kids have been in church all their life. Whatever weekday they were born on, we had them dedicated to God by the very next Sunday. So when I asked them if they could give me the one word I was looking for they felt more than capable enough for the challenge. "Oh you're probably going to talk about love" my son said, "Or giving" my daughter said, "Or joy" my youngest said.

"No" I told them. "They are all great words but they're not the word I'm looking for to describe the master key to the greatest, most abundant living available to us. I'll tell you what, the first of you that can give me the word I'm looking for will get this five dollar note and the offer is open for the next five days."

OUR FIRST PRIORITY

Well, you should have seen my kids go for that money. They were guessing and giving me all kinds of words, some I'd never heard. They had Strong's Concordance and Unger's Bible Dictionary out on the table trying to find that one word. At the end of the week I still had my five dollars. Let me give you this word. I want to introduce it to you in the form of a true story.

Many years ago the great man of God, General William Booth of the Salvation Army, could not attend a meeting of his officers. So in his absence he sent a telegram. In that telegram was one word. As they gathered around and opened it they found this one word written inside;

"Others."

Others.

Living our life focused on others. This is the master key to the most abundant, God-like, living we can do.

Living to give.
Living to serve.
Living to bless.
Living to share.

> *Living our life focused on others. This is the master key to the most abundant, God-like, living we can do.*

This is the heart of God. This is the heart of Jesus.

And, it is the master key to abundant Christian living.

Now we know that Jesus is the key to abundant life. But living to help and serve and bless and share with 'others' is the key to abundant living. There are a lot of Christians who have abundant life through their faith in Christ but they are not enjoying abundant living.

Mark 10:42-44
"Jesus called them together and said, 'You know that those who are regarded as rulers of the Gentiles lord it over them, and their high officials exercise authority over them. Not so with you. Instead, whoever wants to become great among you must be your servant, and whoever wants to be first must be slave of all.'" (NIV)

Jesus came for others. And the day He gave this teaching to His disciples He was trying to teach them something of this master key to abundant living.

OUR FIRST PRIORITY

Dr. Albert Schweitzer
"I don't know what your destiny will be, but one thing I know; the only ones among you who will be really happy are those who will have sought and found how to serve."

> *To the degree your life is swallowed up in the service of others is the degree to which you have truly begun to live.*

To the degree our life is swallowed up in the service of others is the degree to which we have truly begun to live.

The key to abundant living isn't, "What can I get?" but, "What can I give? How can I share? – How can I bless?" Shallow, narrow, empty living says, "What's in it for me?" Rich, deep, fulfilled living says, "What's in it for others?"

Trumbull said,
"People who live for self never succeed in satisfying self or anybody else."

One day Jesus was standing before a bunch

of farmers and gave them this really interesting information:

John 12:24
"Most assuredly, I say to you, unless a grain of wheat falls into the ground and dies, it remains alone; but if it dies, it produces much grain."

Now I'm sure that this astounding truth really shook these farmers. As if they didn't know already that when you put a seed in the ground it would grow!

But the truth is that Jesus was not giving them an agronomy lesson that day. He wasn't talking about a seed at all. He was talking about their life.

I come from Arizona in the USA where we grow a lot of wheat. I've walked through wheat fields and taken the raw stalk in my hands and rubbed the chaff off until I was holding a wheat seed. I have put it in my mouth and eaten it. To be honest with you, the experience is overrated. I noticed several things about the seed. Number one it's small. It's also hard. It's bland. And when you do bite down on it and get it to break so that you can finally chew it, it's not very filling. Actually most of it stayed in my teeth.

But Jesus wasn't really talking about wheat. He was talking about your life and my life. A life focused on itself is just like this wheat; small, hard, bland and unfulfilled.

Many Christians are like the grain of wheat that abides alone – they won't give, they won't share, they won't bless…they won't let go of their pitiful little life. They are Christians but they are dying of boredom.

But others will find the purpose of their life. A seed is meant to be planted and be fruitful and multiply.

If you take one seed and put it in the ground you can get a hundred seeds. If you in turn put that back in the ground you get thousands of seeds. If you then plant all these seeds you would get a farm. If you plant it again you can feed a city, a state, a nation, the world…that's the power of a seed.

But Jesus wasn't talking about a seed, he was talking about your life. He was talking about the power and potential of your life to touch and affect the whole world.

Others…live to give, live to share, live to bless, live to serve. This is the highest level of living available to a man or woman on this planet.

We live in an age of self.

Self-realization – self-actualization – self-promotion – self-assertion – self-expression.
"What's mine is mine and I'll keep it!" "What's yours is mine if I can get my hands on it!" This is the spirit of the age. But it's not the spirit of Jesus.

> *To serve and to give is the highest level of living available to mankind. It is the most God-like thing a man can do.*

Mark 10:45
"For even the Son of Man did not come to be served, but to serve, and to give His life a ransom for many."

To serve and to give is the highest level of living available to mankind. It is the most God-like thing a man can do.

Jesus came for others.
Jesus lived for others.

OUR FIRST PRIORITY

Jesus died for others.

Jesus is seated at the right hand of the Father at this very moment making intercession for others.

Philippians 2:5
"Let this mind be in you which was also in Christ Jesus."

> *The mind of Christ that we are to embrace is the mind of pouring myself out – giving myself up – laying myself down…for others.*

All my life I have understood that the mind of Christ is the mind of an overcomer and victor and that there is no fear or doubt or defeat or lack in the mind of Christ. I know all of this is true. But this is not the context of Philippians 2:5. In this passage the mind of Christ that we are to embrace is the mind of pouring myself out – giving myself up – laying myself down…for others.

This is the mind of serving and giving. This is the mind that says, "How can I die for someone today, what can I give up or lay down for someone else today?" Let this mind be in you.

We must break free from selfishness.

The spirit of this world says, "The more I get the more I've got!" But Jesus says, "The more you give the more you've got."

The world says, "Come on now, you've got to build your little nest egg of security." But Jesus says, "Why don't you just climb up here in my nest and I'll take care of you forever."

There are many Christians today who honestly love the Lord but they don't live to give or bless or share. And I believe that the reason is not because they don't want to. They just have no concept of what true prosperity is.

Prosperity has nothing to do with how much money you make.

> *Prosperity is being secure in your source.*

You and I both know that you can live broke at any level of income. The best definition I have ever heard of prosperity is that prosperity is being secure

OUR FIRST PRIORITY

in your source. If the bank is your source or your job or the government or the share market, then it is obvious that you are not secure. If money is your source, how secure can you be with something that changes value every single day?

But if God is your source, you can be secure. So many of us have a 'Slice of the Pie' mentality. We have become experts on how thin we can slice pie. We've got the grocery slice and the kids-need-new-shoes slice and the tax slice and the tithe slice and my-wife-liked-that-new-dress slice. And so when it comes to giving to missions or the cause of the Great Commission, the real question is, can I get another slice out of this pie? We are already cutting pieces so thin you can see through them.

But let me give you another paradigm. Instead of the 'Slice of the Pie' paradigm why not consider the 'My Father is the Baker' paradigm? If my father is the baker then I could give the whole pie away and still not deplete my resource. If God and His unlimited resources are your source then you can live to give because you are secure in your source.

If God is your source, you can live to bless.

If God is your source, you can live to share.

Paul said in Romans 12:2 that we should not let the world squeeze us into its mold.

The mold of this world is contrary to the Gospel, it is contrary to faith, it is contrary to fulfilled living. Don't let the world dictate to you and your lifestyle! The world is not happy. The world is not enjoying abundant living! Nobody at Melrose Place is happy. Nor is anybody at Beverly Hills 90210 happy either. They are all slim and have trendy haircuts and cute little pouty lips but they're not happy. Why should I let them model my lifestyle for me?

I may just want to change my lifestyle because I love Jesus and because I have found the master key to abundant living.

Get, Get, Get, Take, Take, Take, Mine, Mine, Mine!

Let Jesus fill you with a heart for others.

A self-serving life is so empty, so boring, so unfulfilling. A self-serving marriage or job or church is so dull. The real joy and excitement in living comes in giving. Jesus said, "It is more blessed to give than to receive." (Acts 20:35)

OUR FIRST PRIORITY

According to Jesus we do not measure how blessed we are by what we have or by what we've been given. That's not the measure of a blessed life.

We measure how blessed we are by how much we have released, how much we have given, how much we have shared and served others.

Nathan C. Schaeffer
At the close of life, the question will not be:
how much have you got,
but how much have you given.
Not how much have you won,
but how much have you done.
Not how much have you saved,
but how much have you sacrificed.
Not how much were you honored,
but how much have you served.

Live to bless. It's the master key to a happy life. The more we live for others the less we will live for ourselves. The more we lose ourselves in serving others, the more we will find ourselves in the glory of God.

The Master Key To Abundant Living

Ralph Waldo Emerson

"It is one of the most beautiful compensations of this life that no man can sincerely try to help another without helping himself."

We must lose our life to find it.
We must give to receive.
We must serve to be great.
We must bless to be blessed.
We must comfort to be comforted.
We must share to be significant.
We must assist to succeed.
We must help to be happy.
We must sacrifice to be fulfilled.
We must provide to be satisfied.
We must contribute to be complete.

> *As we focus on other's needs, God will focus on our needs.*

As we focus on other's needs, God will focus on our needs.

If we can believe Philippians 4:19 we can live for others.

OUR FIRST PRIORITY

"And my God shall supply all your need according to His riches in glory by Christ Jesus." (Philippians 4:19 NKJV)

CHAPTER THREE
DRIVING OUT THE MONEY CHANGERS

Driving Out The Money Changers

Mark 11:15-17

"So they came to Jerusalem. And Jesus went into the temple and began to drive out those who bought and sold in the temple, and overturned the tables of the moneychangers and the seats of those who sold doves. And He would not allow anyone to carry wares through the temple. Then He taught, saying to them, 'Is it not written, 'My house shall be called a house of prayer for all nations?' But you have made it a den of thieves.'"

This story has always perplexed me. What was it that caused Jesus such anger? This is the only time in His ministry that He rages with passionate anger. What caused it? Why was He so mad?

We never see Him like this. When the disciples would exasperate Him, He would look to heaven and say, "How long shall I put up with you?" And when the Pharisees would exhaust Him with their hypocrisy, He would say, "You brood of vipers!"

But this is the only time we ever see Him rage with passionate, vehement, white-hot anger.

OUR FIRST PRIORITY

What caused it? What causes Christ to seemingly be so un-Christlike?

> *He raged because the nations were being kept from His house because of the greed of those who dwelt there.*

In verse 17 of Mark 11 Jesus said His house was a house of prayer *for all nations*. I believe He raged because the nations were being kept from His house because of the greed of those who dwelt there. The nations were not being brought into His house because of the pre-occupation of buying and selling and profit.

Gain, prosperity, affluence, wealth and success became the focus and priority of the temple dwellers. And the result was that the nations were left out. He was angry because there was no mercy, or compassion, or sacrifice or caring extended to those outside His house.

Isaiah 56:6-7
"Also the sons of the foreigner who join

themselves to the LORD, to serve Him, and to love the name of the LORD, to be His servants - everyone who keeps from defiling the Sabbath, and holds fast My covenant - even them I will bring to My holy mountain, and make them joyful in My house of prayer. Their burnt offerings and their sacrifices will be accepted on My altar; for My house shall be called a house of prayer for all nations."

Jesus raged because those who had access to His house were more concerned with their prosperity and profit than they were for the least, the lost, and the last outside the Father's house.

We are the wealthiest Christians that have ever lived on the face of the earth. In the western world we make up five per cent of the earth's population and 55 per cent of the earth's wealth. But the scriptures teach us that we can be wealthy and impoverished at the same time.

Psalm 106:14-15
"But [God's people] lusted exceedingly in the wilderness, and tempted God in the desert. And He gave them their request; but sent leanness

OUR FIRST PRIORITY

into their soul." (KJV)

Lusted means to desire, to covet, to wish, to sigh, to want, to be greedy, to crave, to long for, to yearn for.

I know what that feels like every time I walk into a golf store! The truth is we can accumulate much in our life and still be lean in our soul.

John Henry Jowett
"The real measure of our wealth is how much we'd be worth if we lost all our money."

> *We can accumulate much in our life and still be lean in our soul.*

Anonymous
"Measure wealth not by the things you have, but by the things you have for which you would not take money."

Art Buchwald
"The best things in life aren't things."

It's possible to have lots of things and still not have the best things in life.

Revelation 3:17-19
"You say, 'I am rich; I have acquired wealth and do not need a thing.' But you do not realize that you are wretched, pitiful, poor, blind and naked. I counsel you to buy from me gold refined in the fire, so that you can become rich; and white clothes to wear, so that you can cover your shameful nakedness; and salve to put on your eyes, so that you can see. Those whom I love I rebuke and discipline. So be earnest, and repent." (NIV)

Someone has said,
"It is possible to have so much and be worth so little."

Mark Hambourg
"Money is a wonderful thing, but it's possible to pay too high a price for it."

It's sort of like the teacher of a class of second graders in New York who said, "I'll give this five dollar note to the student who can tell me who was the greatest person in the world."
One child said, "It's George Washington."

OUR FIRST PRIORITY

"No, she said, "He's great, but not the greatest."

Another said "Abraham Lincoln". "No, he's great, but not the greatest."

Others suggested John F. Kennedy, Martin Luther King, etc.

A Jewish boy in the class raised his hand and said, "Jesus Christ". The teacher gave the child the five dollar note, but said, "How is it that you, a Jewish boy, said 'Jesus?' "

He said, "In my heart it is Moses, but business is business."

So I guess we can sometimes pay too high a price for money!

> *A man's treatment of money is the most decisive test of his character – how he makes it and how he spends it.*

James Moffatt

"A man's treatment of money is the most decisive test of his character – how he makes it and how he spends it."

Proverbs 13:7

"There is one who makes

himself rich, yet has nothing…"

George W. Truett, a well-known pastor in Texas, was invited to dinner in the home of a very wealthy man. After the meal, the host led him to a place where they could get a good view of the surrounding area. Pointing to the oil wells punctuating the landscape, he boasted, "Twenty-five years ago I had nothing. Now, as far as you can see, it's all mine." Looking in the opposite direction at his sprawling fields of grain, he said, "That's all mine too."

Turning east toward huge herds of cattle, he bragged, "They're all mine."

Then pointing to the west and a beautiful forest, he exclaimed, "That too is all mine."

He paused, expecting Dr. Truett to compliment him on his great success. Pastor Truett, however, placing one hand on the man's shoulder and pointing heavenward with the other, simply said, "How much do you have in that direction?" The man hung his head and confessed, "I've never thought of that."

Life is so tragic for the person who has plenty to live on, but nothing to live for.

OUR FIRST PRIORITY

Friends, Jesus gave us a mission to live for, and the mission is that the nations outside of His house do not perish! His house is to be called a house of prayer for all nations. He is not willing that any should perish but that all should come to repentance.

John 3:16
"For God so loved the world that He gave His only begotten Son that whoever believes in Him should not perish but have everlasting life."

Romans 10:13-15
"For whoever calls on the name of the Lord shall be saved. How then shall they call on Him in whom they have not believed? And how shall they believe in Him of whom they have not heard? And how shall they hear without a preacher? And how shall they preach unless they are sent?"

And how can they be sent if we prize our possessions above proclaiming peace to perishing people?
This is what caused Jesus' rage.

The temple dwellers were living for temporal treasures at the expense of eternal souls and perishing nations.

> The temple dwellers were living for temporal treasures at the expense of eternal souls and perishing nations.

If we have as our prominent priority our private property, and if our primary preference is our personal possessions, how will we ever propel passionate preachers to proclaim pardon to perishing people?

We read of this account again in the Gospel of John.

John 2:14-16
"And He found in the temple those who sold oxen and sheep and doves, and the moneychangers doing business. When He had made a whip of cords, He drove them all out of the temple, with the sheep and the oxen, and poured out the changers' money and overturned the tables…and He said to those who sold

doves, 'Take these things away! Do not make My Father's house a house of merchandise!'"

In the western world, where we have so much of the world's wealth, God forbid that the primary focus of our money is merchandise.

If you live in the west, the rest of the world automatically thinks you are rich. Half of the earth's population lives on $1.50 a day! And so by that standard we are all rich.

1 Timothy 6:17-19
"Command those who are rich in this present [western] world not to be arrogant nor to put their hope in wealth, which is so uncertain, but to put their hope in God, who richly provides us with everything for our enjoyment. Command them to do good, to be rich in good deeds, and to be generous and willing to share. In this way they will lay up treasure for themselves as a firm foundation for the coming age, so that they may take hold of the life that is truly life." (NIV)

Aesop's fable
"The true value of money is not in its

possession but in its use."

> *Christians show what they are by what they do with what they have.*

Christians show what they are by what they do with what they have.

Joseph Addison said he saw these words on a gravestone: "What I spent I lost; what I possessed is left to others; what I gave away remains with me."

Jim Elliott
"No man is a fool who gives up what he cannot keep to gain what he cannot lose."

Charles Stanley
"Each of us will eventually give away all our earthly possessions. How we choose to do so, however, is a reflection of our commitment to the Kingdom of God."

Edgar A. Guest
Out of this life I shall never take
Things of silver and gold I make

OUR FIRST PRIORITY

All that I cherish and hoard away
After I leave, on earth must stay.
Though I have toiled for a painting rare
To hang on my wall I must leave it there.
Though I call it mine and boast of its worth
I must give it up when I quit the earth.
All that I gather and all that I keep,
I must leave behind when I fall asleep.
And I often wonder what I shall own
In that other life, when I pass alone.
What shall they find and what shall they see
In the soul that answers the call for me?
Shall the great judge learn when my task
 is through
That the spirit had gathered some riches too?
Or shall at the last it be mine to find
That all I had worked for I'd left behind?

> *No man is a fool who gives up what he cannot keep to gain what he cannot lose.*

Matthew 6:20-21
"…but lay up for yourselves treasures in heaven, where neither moth nor rust destroys and where thieves do not break in and steal.

For where your treasure is, there your heart will be also."

The body of David Livingstone is buried in England where he was born, but his heart was buried in the Africa he loved. At the foot of a tall tree in a small African village the natives dug a hole and placed in it the heart of this man whom they loved and respected. If your heart were to be buried in the place you loved most during life, where would it be? Would it be in an appropriate space down at the office? Or maybe at the soccer club or Rotary or at the mall or the plaza? Or possibly down at the bank? Where would they bury your heart?

Jesus made a whip and drove men and women out of His Father's house. Do you know why? Because their attitude toward money was keeping the nations out.

Let us use our resources to open wide the doors of the Father's house to many nations.

Let us who are the most blessed people in the world, actually the most blessed people in history; let us use our blessings to bless the families of the earth.

God told Abraham:

Genesis 12:3
"I will bless those who bless you, and I will curse him who curses you; and in you all the families of the earth shall be blessed."

And then the Apostle Paul told us:

Galatians 3:29
"And if you are Christ's, then you are Abraham's seed, and heirs according to the promise."

The promise to Abraham was that he would be blessed and that he would be a blessing to all the families of the earth.

Christopher Winans, in his book, *Malcolm Forbes: The Man Who Had Everything,* tells of a motorcycle tour that Forbes took through Egypt in 1984 with his Capitalist Tool motorcycle team. After viewing the staggering burial tomb of King Tut, Forbes seemed to be in a reflective mood. As they were returning to the hotel in a shuttle bus, Forbes turned to one of his associates and asked with all sincerity, "Do you think I'll be remembered after I die?"

Well of course Forbes is remembered. He is remembered as the man who coined the phrase, "He who dies with the most toys wins." This was the wisdom of Malcolm Forbes. In fact, it was his ambition. That's why he collected scores of motorcycles. That's why he would pay over a million dollars for a Fabergé egg. That's why he owned castles, hot air balloons and countless other toys he can no longer access.

The Lord Jesus Christ gave us words of superior wisdom when He said,

> *The only way to win in death is to do the will of God in life.*

Matthew 16:26
"What good will it be for a man if he gains the whole world, yet forfeits his soul?" (NIV)

It is a fatally deficient wisdom that declares "He who dies with the most toys wins." The truth is he who dies with the most toys still dies. And friend, the only way to

OUR FIRST PRIORITY

win in death is to do the will of God in life.

Revelation 18:11-17
"And the merchants of the earth will weep and mourn over her, for no one buys their merchandise anymore: merchandise of gold and silver, precious stones and pearls, fine linen and purple, silk and scarlet, every kind of citron wood, every kind of object of ivory, every kind of object of most precious wood, bronze, iron, and marble; and cinnamon and incense, fragrant oil and frankincense, wine and oil, fine flour and wheat, cattle and sheep, horses and chariots, and bodies and souls of men. *The fruit that your soul longed for has gone from you, and all the things which are rich and splendid have gone from you, and you shall find them no more at all*. The merchants of these things, who became rich by her, will stand at a distance for fear of her torment, weeping and wailing, and saying, '*Alas, alas, that great city that was clothed in fine linen, purple, and scarlet, and adorned with gold and precious stones and pearls! For in one hour such great riches came to nothing.*'"

The Bible speaks of a day when all the riches of the world will come to nothing in one hour. May we be wise and invest our temporal treasures in that which will accomplish eternal good.

The one thing we cannot do about missions is rid ourselves of our responsibility.

Henry Martyn
"The Spirit of Christ is the spirit of missions, and the nearer we get to Him the more intensely missionary we must become."

CHAPTER FOUR
KNOWING WHY YOU HAVE WHAT YOU HAVE

Knowing Why You Have What You Have

Esther had it all!

There was a king, Ahasuerus, who had a drunken party for a bunch of leaders who were all men. And it went on for days, and they began to talk about everything that men in drunkenness would talk about. Somehow, eventually the conversation got around to women. The king evidently began to brag about the beauty of his wife, Queen Vashti. She was a magnificent queen. So in this drunken debauchery, the guests said, "Bring her out so we can have a look at her". So word was sent to the queen, "Come out, the men want to have a look at you. The king requests your presence. Come out looking good, wear that new jumper you bought at Sachs 5th Ave, and just come out looking really, really nice." Now Queen Vashti had such a sense of dignity and self-respect she said, "No. I am not going out there".

Well, word came back to the king, and the servants said, "Your majesty, she said n..n..n.. actually what she said was nnn... no." And I am sure in my imagination that when that report was given, the whole banquet, the whole party stopped and you could have heard a pin drop. And all the eyes of the men turned to the king.

"Your majesty, can she say that? What if all the women in your kingdom hear of this?" And fear gripped the heart of every man. What if all women learnt how to use that word and say, 'no'. So the king banished her and sent her away from his sight forever.

Now, what a stupid king. He had this beautiful wife with dignity, but in a drunken state he lost her. So now the queen's position is vacant. They search for a new queen, and they parade all of the beautiful women before this king. And out of all of them Esther was chosen. A beauty. She was actually a captive, a Jewish girl but the king did not know this. Her grace and beauty overwhelmed him and he took her to be his wife.

Imagine little Esther. She has gone from a captive to a queen, from poverty to the penthouse. Her God-given beauty has distinguished her from thousands of young women. Can you just see her there in the royal palace, brushing her marvelous thick black hair? The best of everything in life had become hers.

A vast wardrobe, untold wealth, servants who wait to fulfill her every whim.

I imagine her standing in front of her amazing wardrobe and saying what every woman says when she stands in front of her closet, "I don't have a thing to wear!"

My wife says that she only has two complaints: nothing to wear and no place to put it in the closet.

The hand of God was on Esther to elevate her to a place of power and prestige and prominence.

What she had was amazing!
What she had was unbelievable!
What she had was incredible!
What she had could very easily seduce her into forgetting why she had it!

Esther is a picture of the Church today. She is rich, she is increased with goods, she has need of nothing. Through Jesus' poverty she has become rich!

By the standard of the rest of the world, what we have, how we live, what we own

OUR FIRST PRIORITY

and possess….is almost unthinkable!

Half of the earth's population lives on $1.50 a day.

What we have is the blessing of the King.

What we have is access to all He possesses.

What we have is a God who meets all our needs according to His riches in glory by Christ Jesus.

What we have can easily seduce us into forgetting why we have it! 'What' and 'why' are two words which hold life and death. When you live by the 'what' you can only see blessings and possessions as ends in themselves.

The western world is in a race to see 'what' more we can accumulate before we die. Like the bumper sticker I saw on the back of a Ford Bronco that said, "He who dies with the most toys wins."

> *'What' we have can easily seduce us into forgetting 'why' we have it*

You never see a U-Haul trailer behind a hearse.

In Revelation 3, the Laodicean church was rich and increased with goods and had need of nothing. That's 'what' she had. All her needs were met.

But she forgot 'why' she had it!

Jesus said she didn't even know she was wretched, miserable, poor, blind and naked. She forgot why she had what she had!

Jesus said to her, "I love you, therefore I rebuke you."

What Esther had was beauty, wealth, possessions, position and comfort. Why she had it was to deliver a nation!

She took what she had and laid it on the altar to go to the King and plead for the Jews.

Esther 4:13 & 14
"Then Mordecai told them to answer Esther: 'Do not think in your heart that you will escape in the king's palace any more than all the other Jews. For if you remain completely silent at this time, relief and deliverance will arise for the Jews from another place, but you and your father's house will perish. Yet who knows whether you have come to the kingdom for such a time as this?'"

What Mordecai told Esther applies to us

OUR FIRST PRIORITY

today. God is going to do something marvelous. He is going to accomplish His Word, He is going to harvest the earth and He is going to do it with us or without us.

If we do not rise up and obey Him and fulfill the Great Commission then He will raise up someone else to do it. Help and deliverance will come from some place else because somewhere, somehow, some way, someone is going to do it.

His plan will not fail.

A great deal of the Church is all dressed up with nowhere to go! All dressed up, but no sense of destiny!

We are drowning in what, for lack of why.
Why are we so blessed?
Why have we been baptized with the Holy Spirit?

Why have we been given so much?

> *We are drowning in what, for lack of why.*

It's frightening to think anyone could be empowered for such a time as this only to hoard it.

Knowing Why You Have What You Have

We see this illustrated in:

2 Kings 6:24
"And it happened after this that Ben-Hadad king of Syria gathered all his army, and went up and besieged Samaria."

In this story we see four lepers who sat starving outside the gates of Samaria. There was incredible famine inside the city, so they rose up and headed for the Syrian camp. As they approached, God sent a roar into the camp which melted the soldier's hearts. They literally ran in terror and left a feast of riches totally intact. So the lepers entered the deserted camp.

All of a sudden they were no longer dying, starving lepers. Now they were stuffed, rich and dressed to the hilt. They began to bury treasure, put on fancy clothes and have food fights!

But somewhere in the midst of all the glory and blessing, their hearts enriched by what they had, they began to consider why they had it!

2 Kings 7:9
"Then said they to each other, 'We're not doing

OUR FIRST PRIORITY

right. This is a day of good news and we are keeping it to ourselves. If we wait until daylight, punishment will overtake us. Let's go at once and report this to the royal palace.'"

They realized the 'why' of the 'what' they had received. Have we? Have you and I realized why we have what we have?

I tell you, the Holy Spirit is in you for such a time as this! The blessings of God are on you, me and on our nation for such a time as this!

There is nothing more tragic and heartbreaking than a people without a purpose, people without a why.

> *There is nothing more tragic and heartbreaking than a people without a purpose.*

We see this whole concept illustrated again in the book of Exodus. Here the children of Israel are leaving Egypt. They have been slaves for 400 years and now they are leaving with the wealth of Egypt!

Exodus 12:35 - 36
"And the people of Israel did as Moses said and

asked the Egyptians for silver and gold jewelry and for clothing. And the Lord gave the Israelites favor with the Egyptians so that they gave them whatever they wanted. And the Egyptians were practically stripped of everything they owned!" (TLB)

God blessed His people. We see the blessings: the 'what' that He gave them - gold, silver, garments and all the wealth of Egypt! We know 'what' they had, but 'why' did they have it?

The answer is found in Exodus 24, when God called Moses up to the top of Mt Sinai. He went up into the glory of God for 40 days and 40 nights! There he got a word from God and he's going back down the mountain to deliver it.

Now get ready folks! This is going to be good! Forty days and forty nights in the presence of Almighty God! How many of us would be listening and excited to hear what a man of God had to say after being in His literal, physical presence and audibly transcribing the message?

OUR FIRST PRIORITY

"Moses! What is the word of the Lord? What is God saying?"

Exodus 25:1 - 2
"Then the LORD spoke to Moses, saying: 'Speak to the children of Israel, that they bring Me an offering. From everyone who gives it willingly with his heart you shall take My offering.'"

What? Bring an offering to God? Give? Forty days and forty nights in the Shekinah glory of God and he comes down from the mountain and preaches on giving! You've got to be kidding!

But in verse 10 we see that their offering would build the Ark of the Covenant. God's literal and physical presence would dwell between the wings of the two Cherubim on the top of the Ark. The priests would pick up the Ark of the Covenant and carry it on their shoulders. They would carry the Ark of His Presence. So the children of Israel's offering would literally take the presence of God into the nations…into Godless, heathen, and pagan nations!

This is why God blessed His people.
Look at what God gave them.
Look at why He gave it.

Their destiny was to partner with God through their giving and in so doing bring His presence into the nations of Moab, Philistia and Amon.

Our destiny is to bring the presence of God into the nations of Asia, Eastern Europe, Africa and Latin America, through the Gospel of the Lord Jesus Christ!

A Christian life centered in what (we have) is unfulfilling and unproductive.

A life centered in why (we have it) will fulfill its purpose with an excitement and sense of destiny. We have so much. Like

> *Our destiny is to bring the presence of God into the nations of Asia, Eastern Europe, Africa and Latin America!*

OUR FIRST PRIORITY

Esther, we were born and blessed for such a time as this!

> What you have is your life!
> Why you have it is for the glory of God!

CHAPTER FIVE
WILL GOD'S WILL BE DONE?

Genesis 24:1-5

"Now Abraham was old, well advanced in age; and the LORD had blessed Abraham in all things. So Abraham said to the oldest servant of his house, who ruled over all that he had, 'Please, put your hand under my thigh, and I will make you swear by the LORD, the God of heaven and the God of the earth, that you will not take a wife for my son from the daughters of the Canaanites, among whom I dwell; but you shall go to my country and to my family, and take a wife for my son Isaac.' And the servant said to him, 'Perhaps the woman *will not be willing* to follow me to this land. Must I take your son back to the land from which you came?'"

Here was the plan. The purpose of God was being thought out and strategized. There was only one problem...what if the key player, the woman, was not willing?

This whole thing was resting on her.

She would be the wife of Isaac, the mother of Jacob, the mother of Israel. David would come from her offspring. Eventually the

OUR FIRST PRIORITY

Lord Jesus would come to this planet through her lineage.

But what if she was not willing?
What if she didn't want to go?
What if she didn't want to leave?
What if she didn't want to fulfill her purpose and destiny?

One of the most remarkable things about being a human being is our amazing power of free will and choice. We are like God Himself in this attribute.

Alfred A. Montapert
"Every person has free choice. Free to obey or disobey the Natural Laws. Your choice determines the consequences. Nobody ever did, or ever will, escape the consequences of his choices."

> *We all have freedom of choice but we do not have freedom of consequences*

Eric Allenbaugh, American author of *Wake-Up Calls*.
"Every choice moves us

closer to or farther away from something. Where are your choices taking your life?"

Edgar A. Guest
You are the person who has to decide.
Whether you'll do it or toss it aside;
You are the person who makes up your mind.
Whether you'll lead or will linger behind
Whether you'll try for the goal that's afar.
Or just be contented to stay where you are.

Genesis 24:8
"And if the woman is not willing to follow you, then you will be released from this oath..."

God's purposes ride upon the willing hearts of His people.

How is God's will done in the earth? Jesus prayed for it, "Thy will be done on earth as it is in heaven." How is His will done? It's done when we say with King David:

Psalm 40:8
"I delight to do Your will, O my God, and Your law is within my heart."

OUR FIRST PRIORITY

Acts 13:22
"… 'I have found David the son of Jesse, a man after My own heart, who will do all My will."

God's will is done when we say with the Lord Jesus:

John 4:34
"My food is to do the will of Him who sent Me, and to finish His work."

God's will is done by willing people. When my will is to do His will, His will is done.

> *God's will is done by willing people. When my will is to do His will, His will is done.*

Mark 3:35
"For whoever does the will of God is My brother and My sister and mother."

Matthew 7:21
"Not everyone who says to Me, 'Lord, Lord,' shall enter the kingdom of heaven, but he who does the will of My Father in heaven."

Will God's Will Be Done?

And what is the will of God?

John 6:40
"And this is the will of Him who sent Me, that everyone…may have everlasting life; and I will raise him up at the last day."

2 Peter 3:9
"The Lord is not…willing that any should perish but that all should come to repentance."

> *We must realize that you and I are now the major players in the plan of redemption.*

To the degree you are willing that none should perish, is the degree to which God's will, will be done. We must realize that you and I are now the major players in the plan of redemption. God's part of the work is done. He gave His only begotten Son.

Christ's part of the work is done. He said on the cross, "It is finished."

Your work is still to be done. Are you willing?

OUR FIRST PRIORITY

God's work of redemption is done – it's just waiting to be delivered.

Mark 16:15
"And He said to them, 'Go into all the world and preach the Gospel to every creature.'"

Is that your plan? It's God's plan for you. Are you willing? Or is this contrary to your plans?

Abraham's servant said, "What if the woman is not willing?"

What if she won't leave?

What if she's full of fear?

What if she's self-absorbed?

What if she's self-focused?

What if she's not willing to move out of her comfort zone?

Will God's message get delivered to a lost and dying world?

Luke 14:23
"Then the master said to the servant, 'Go out into the highways and hedges, and compel them to come in, that my house may be filled.'"

Will His house be full? Will the message that they're invited be delivered?

Or will they go through life never knowing that there was a God who loved them and invited them in…because the message never got delivered.

The reason it never got delivered is because those who were commissioned to deliver it were not willing.

John 15:16
"You did not choose Me, but I chose you and appointed you that you should go and bear fruit…"

John 20:21
"So Jesus said to them again, 'Peace to you! As the Father has sent Me, I also send you.'"

You are such a vital part of His plan! Without you delivering the good news, it's the same as if there were no good news. What good is Christ dying on the cross for the sins of the world if the world doesn't know about it?

OUR FIRST PRIORITY

What good is a declaration of pardon to a condemned prisoner if the news of the pardon never reaches him?

What good is God loving the world so much that He gave His only begotten Son that whosoever believes in Him should not perish but have everlasting life...if that message never reaches the perishing people?

What good is Christ dying on the cross for the sins of the world if the world doesn't know about it?

Some years ago I remember watching the movie 'Gallipoli' starring Mel Gibson. I was interested in the movie because it is such an important part of Australian history. What I remember most is the opening scene and the closing scene.

In the opening scene we see a young Aussie athlete training out on some bush in the middle of nowhere in the early morning hours. We see him crouched down in the starting position talking to himself. He's saying, "My legs are like steel springs. I'm going to run as fast as a leopard."

And then his old crusty coach at the other end of the bush track fires the starting pistol and off he goes.

In the closing scenes of the movie we see that same young man along with his regiment in the trenches of Gallipoli. Hundreds and hundreds of Australian troops have been charging out of the trenches and they are being mowed down and killed by enemy fire. Wave after disastrous wave meet with the same fate and by now bodies are lying on top of bodies. Every new wave that goes cannot get any further than the last group and it is madness and mayhem to keep sending the boys into certain death. But the communications are down. The Generals don't seem to realize the absolute futility of continuing the assault.

The character Mel Gibson plays has the assignment of trying to reach the command post to have the order to keep going over the trenches rescinded. Now he is on his way back with the order to stop the insanity and massacre. He now has the word that will save the lives of all his mates. They don't have to perish; they don't have to go over the wall and die. So now he is racing to get this life saving message to his men in time. In the movie he is running as fast as he can, leaping over obstacles and straining to reach them before it's too late.

Back in the trench they don't know that the order to charge has been withdrawn and so they prepare to go over the wall. The young athlete, who was in the opening scene of the movie, takes his racing medals off his neck and hangs them on his bayonet. He places the palm of his hands on the dirt walls and prepares to charge into the machine guns. He starts talking to himself saying, "My legs are like steel springs. I'm going to run like a leopard."

I remember the sadness I felt when the Sergeant gave the command for them all to charge. Over the wall they went to their death. Mel Gibson's character heard them go just as he was arriving and fell to the ground screaming, "No!"

He had the message of life but it did not reach them in time.

How will others know if you're not willing to go?

Will God's Will Be Done?

> *How will others know if you're not willing to go?*
> *How will others live if you're not willing to give?*

How will others live if you're not willing to give?

John 17:18
"As You sent Me into the world, I also have sent them into the world."

Will God's will be done?

Robert Schuller
"If it's to be it's up to me!"

Will the message get through – it's up to you. What if the woman in Genesis was not willing?

Genesis 24:8-20
"'And if the woman is not willing to follow you, then you will be released from this oath; only do not take my son back there.'

"So the servant put his hand under the thigh of Abraham his master, and swore to him concerning this matter. Then the servant took ten of his master's camels and departed, for all his

OUR FIRST PRIORITY

> *Will the message get through – it's up to you.*

master's goods were in his hand. And he arose and went to Mesopotamia, to the city of Nahor. And he made his camels kneel down outside the city by a well of water at evening time, the time when women go out to draw water.

"Then he said, 'O Lord God of my master Abraham, please give me success this day, and show kindness to my master Abraham. Behold, I stand here by the well of water, and the daughters of the men of the city are coming out to draw water. Now let it be that the young woman to whom I say, 'Please let down your pitcher that I may drink,' and she says, 'Drink, and I will also give your camels a drink'- let her be the one You have appointed for Your servant Isaac. And by this I will know that You have shown kindness to my master Abraham'… And it happened, before he had finished speaking, that behold, Rebekah, who was born to Bethuel, son of Milcah, the wife of Nahor, Abraham's brother, came out with her pitcher on her shoulder. Now the young woman was very beautiful to behold, a virgin; no man had known her. And she went down to the well, filled her pitcher, and came up. And the servant ran to meet her and said, 'Please let me drink a little water from your pitcher.' So she said, 'Drink, my lord.' Then she quickly let her pitcher down to her hand, and gave him a drink. And when she had finished giving him a drink, she said, 'I will draw water for your camels also, until they have finished drinking.' Then she quickly emptied her pitcher into the trough, ran back to the well to draw water, and drew for all his camels."

She was willing!

Genesis 24:54-58
"Then they arose in the morning, and Abraham's servant said, 'Send me away to my master.'
But her [Rebekah] brother and her mother said, 'Let the young woman stay with us a few days, at least ten; after that she may go.'
And he said to them, 'Do not hinder me, since the LORD has prospered my way; send me away so that I may go to my master.'

OUR FIRST PRIORITY

So they said, 'We will call the young woman and ask her personally.'
Then they called Rebekah and said to her, 'Will you go with this man?' And she said, 'I will go.'"

Because she's willing, the plan of God will not fail.

Because she's willing, the purpose of God will prevail.

Because she was willing to give and because she was willing to go she would become a channel through which the Messiah would come to the world.

If you and I are willing to give and to go, the good news of the Messiah will be delivered to a dying and desperate world.

Rebekah was willing and eager. She was so generous and diligent. Each camel drank 60 liters of water. She gave and she gave. She gave with joy and enthusiasm. She was eager to bless and share and give and refresh and serve.

What a woman!

She was doing the will of God!

She saw herself as a channel of blessing.

Will God's Will Be Done?

She was refreshing a stranger and lifting a burden.

She had no idea that those camels were loaded with treasure for her!

She had no idea that the camels she was watering were hers! The very act of her willingness made the camels and all they carried hers.

She watered them and they benefited her!

She refreshed them and they refreshed her!

She blessed them and they blessed her! She gave to them and they gave back to her, pressed down, shaken together and running over.

Proverbs 11:25
"The generous soul will be made rich, and he who waters will also be watered himself."

Matthew 19:29
"And everyone who has left houses or brothers or sisters or father or mother or children or fields for my sake will receive a hundred times as much and will inherit eternal life." (NIV)

The greatest thing you can do for you is give

OUR FIRST PRIORITY

> *The greatest thing you can do for you is give yourself up and do the will of God.*

yourself up and do the will of God.

Have you found the joy and wonder of giving and sharing and being generous?

Jayne Fisher watched anxiously as her 17-year-old daughter Katie pulled her unruly lamb into the arena of the Madison County Junior Livestock sale. With luck, Katie wouldn't collapse, as she had during a livestock show the day before.

Katie was battling cancer. This was her first chance in months to be outdoors having fun, away from hospitals and chemotherapy treatments, and she had come with high hopes for earning some sizeable spending money.

She had wavered a little on her decision to part with the lamb, but with the price of lamb averaging two dollars a pound, Katie was looking forward to a lot more than pocket money. So she presented the lamb for viewing, and the bidding began.

That's when Roger Wilson, the auctioneer, had a sudden inspiration that brought some unexpected results.

"We sort of let folks know that Katie had a situation that wasn't too pleasant," is how he tells it. He hoped that his introduction would push the bidding up, at least a little bit.

Well, the lamb sold for US$11.50 a pound, but things didn't stop there. The buyer paid up, then decided to give the lamb back so that it could be sold again.

That started a chain reaction, with families buying the animal and giving it back, over and over again. When local businesses started buying and returning, the earnings really began to pile up. The first sale is the only one Katie's mom remembers. After that, she was crying too hard as the crowd kept shouting, "Resell! Resell!"

Katie's lamb was sold 36 times that day, and the last buyer gave it back for good.

Katie ended up with more than US$10,000 for a fund to pay her medical expenses - and she still got to keep her famous lamb.

OUR FIRST PRIORITY

Has your heart been enlarged with the greatness of giving or has it shriveled up from being focused on yourself?

Acts 20:35
"…The Lord Jesus said, 'It is more blessed to give than to receive.'"

> *Has your heart been enlarged with the greatness of giving or has it shriveled up from being focused on yourself?*

Will God's will be done? Will the message get delivered to the 1.5 billion people who have never yet heard of the name of Jesus?

What if the woman who has the message, what if the woman who is the key to the plan of God, what if the woman who is the espoused bride of the Lord Jesus Christ, is not willing?

What if she won't go? What if she won't send? What if the focus of her time and money is the temporal and not the eternal, the earthly and not the heavenly?

Will God's Will Be Done?

Ezekiel 3:18-19
"When I say to the wicked, 'You shall surely die,' and you give him no warning, nor speak to warn the wicked from his wicked way, to save his life, that same wicked man shall die in his iniquity; but his blood I will require at your hand. Yet, if you warn the wicked, and he does not turn from his wickedness, nor from his wicked way, he shall die in his iniquity; but you have delivered your soul."

> Delivering the message delivers me.
> Releasing others releases me.
> Rescuing others rescues me.
> Liberating others liberates me.
> Refreshing others refreshes me.
> Helping others helps me.

Matthew 10:39-40
"If your first concern is to look after yourself, you'll never find yourself. But if you forget about yourself and look to me, you'll find both yourself and me. We are intimately linked in this harvest work." (The Message)

OUR FIRST PRIORITY

Matthew 16:25

"Self-help is no help at all. Self-sacrifice is the way, my way, to finding yourself, your true self." (The Message)

If Rebekah would have been self-absorbed she would have prolonged and thwarted and hindered and delayed the will of God.

We are responsible for delivering the message.

We must take the message or send the message.

2 Corinthians 5:18-20

"God put the world square with Himself through the Messiah, giving the world a fresh start by offering forgiveness of sins. God has given us the task of telling everyone what He is doing. We're Christ's representatives. God uses us to persuade men and women…" (The Message)

Let us be like Rebekah - willing. If she hadn't been willing, the consequences would have been devastating.

> *What will be the consequences if we are not willing to deliver this message?*

What will be the consequences if we are not willing to deliver this message? Let us go or let us give.

Will God's will be done? Will all have eternal life? Will none perish?

It's up to you. It's up to me.

CHAPTER SIX
THE COMPASSION TO DELIVER NATIONS

The Compassion To Deliver Nations

Exodus 2:1-6

"And a man of the house of Levi went and took as wife a daughter of Levi. So the woman conceived and bore a son. And when she saw that he was a beautiful child, she hid him three months. But when she could no longer hide him, she took an ark of bulrushes for him, daubed it with asphalt and pitch, put the child in it, and laid it in the reeds by the river's bank. And his sister stood afar off, to know what would be done to him. Then the daughter of Pharaoh came down to bathe at the river. And her maidens walked along the riverside; and when she saw the ark among the reeds, she sent her maid to get it. And when she had opened it, she saw the child, and behold, the baby wept. So she had compassion on him, and said, 'This is one of the Hebrews' children.'"

How different the story of Moses and the deliverance of the Hebrew children would be if it were not for the compassion of this woman.

Her caring, her mercy, her selflessness was literally the saving of a nation. Her act of kindness triggered the events that led to the

OUR FIRST PRIORITY

deliverance of a nation. God's plan was accomplished through her compassion. That is how God's plan is accomplished today.

Compassion is the force that will move us to get the Gospel to nations.

Matthew 9:36-38
"But when He saw the multitudes, He was moved with compassion for them, because they were weary and scattered, like sheep having no shepherd. Then He said to His disciples, 'The harvest truly is plentiful, but the laborers are few. Therefore pray the Lord of the harvest to send out laborers into His harvest.'"

He saw, He felt, He was moved to action.

> *Compassion is the force that will move us to get the Gospel to nations.*

The difference between compassion and sentiment is:

Compassion moves us,
Sentiment soothes us.

Many Christians today are much more into being soothed than being moved.

The Compassion To Deliver Nations

> *Many Christians today are much more into being soothed than being moved.*

Compassion moves.
Compassion brings action.

Until you and I are moved with the same compassion that moved the Lord Jesus, the multitudes will continue to be weary and scattered and be sheep without the Shepherd.

Until you and I care and have mercy, the harvest of souls will continue to go unharvested.

Jesus said go, give, deliver the message, but we won't go and we won't give if we don't care.

Compassion is the force that will cause us to spend and be spent for others. Caring moves us to go and to give so that others can live.

Luke 10:30
"Then Jesus answered and said: 'A certain man went down from Jerusalem to Jericho, and fell among thieves, who stripped him of his clothing, wounded him, and departed, leaving him half dead.'"

OUR FIRST PRIORITY

This is a fairly accurate description of the condition of every man in every nation.

John 10:10
"The thief [the devil] does not come except to steal, and to kill, and to destroy. I have come that they may have life, and that they may have it more abundantly."

Luke 10:31-32
"Now by chance a certain priest came down that road. And when he saw him, he passed by on the other side. Likewise a Levite, when he arrived at the place, came and looked, and passed by on the other side."

What the priest and Levite had going for them was a calling, an anointing, an office, a ministry, education, blessing, prosperity, and respect…but all those things were not enough to move them to make a difference in this perishing man's life.

Verses 33-34
"But a certain Samaritan, as he journeyed, came

where he was. And when he saw him, he had compassion. So he went to him and bandaged his wounds, pouring on oil and wine; and he set him on his own animal, brought him to an inn, and took care of him."

He had compassion so he went to him. Compassion moved him. He cared. It cost him. Saving others is costly. Caring is costly.

So is not caring...

The story is told of Sadhu Sundar Singh and a companion who were traveling through a pass high in the Himalayan Mountains. At one point they came across a body lying in the snow. Sundar Singh wished to stop and help the unfortunate man, but his companion refused, saying, "We shall lose our lives if we burden ourselves with him."

But Sundar Singh would not think of leaving the man to die in the ice and snow. As his companion bade him farewell, Sundar Singh lifted the poor traveler onto his back. With great exertion on his part, he bore the man onward,

> *Caring is costly.*
> *So is not caring...*

OUR FIRST PRIORITY

but gradually the heat from Sundar Singh's body, which increased the more he exerted, began to warm up the poor frozen fellow, and he revived. Soon both were walking together side by side. Catching up with his former companion, they found him dead - frozen by the cold.

In the case of Sundar Singh, he was willing to lose his life on behalf of another, and in the process found it; in the case of his uncaring companion, he sought to save his life but lost it.

The Samaritan saved two lives that day.

As he valued the perishing man's life his own life increased with value.

The Priest and the Levite, who were God's servants, had no compassion so they didn't go to him. They didn't care. They didn't help. They did not value this man's life above their own convenience and comfort. But it cost them.

I tell you not caring is more costly than caring.

> *I tell you not caring is more costly than caring.*

Matthew 25: 31-46
"When he finally arrives, blazing in beauty and all his angels with

him, the Son of Man will take his place on his glorious throne. Then all the nations will be arranged before Him and he will sort the people out, much as a shepherd sorts out sheep and goats, putting sheep to his right and goats to his left.

"Then the King will say to those on his right, 'Enter, you who are blessed by my Father! Take what's coming to you in this kingdom. It's been ready for you since the world's foundation. And here's why:

I was hungry and you fed me,
I was thirsty and you gave me a drink,
I was homeless and you gave me a room,
I was shivering and you gave me clothes,
I was sick and you stopped to visit,
I was in prison and you came to me.'

"Then those 'sheep' are going to say, 'Master, what are you talking about? When did we ever see you hungry and feed you, thirsty and give you a drink? And when did we ever see you sick or in prison and come to you?' Then the King will say, 'I'm telling the solemn truth: Whenever you did one of these things to someone overlooked or ignored, that was me—you did it to me.'

"Then he will turn to the 'goats,' the ones on his left, and say, 'Get out, worthless goats! You're good for nothing but the fires of hell. And why? Because -
I was hungry and you gave me no meal,
I was thirsty and you gave me no drink,
I was homeless and you gave me no bed,
I was shivering and you gave me no clothes,
Sick and in prison, and you never visited.'

"Then those 'goats' are going to say, 'Master, what are you talking about? When did we ever see you hungry or thirsty or homeless or shivering or sick or in prison and didn't help?' He will answer them, 'I'm telling the solemn truth: Whenever you failed to do one of these things to someone who was being overlooked or ignored, that was me - you failed to do it to me.' Then those 'goats' will be herded to their eternal doom, but the 'sheep' to their eternal reward."
(The Message)

The Priest and the Levite were afraid of losing their time, their income, their convenience, their comfort. But what they lost was their soul.

Christianity is all about compassion and caring and selflessness and those things cost us.

Not having those things cost us even more!

When we stand before Jesus, He's not going to ask what kind of car you drove – He's going to ask what did you do for the helpless?

He's not going to ask what kind of clothes you wore – He's going to ask who did you help clothe?

He's not going to ask if you ate in fancy restaurants – He's going to ask if you fed the hungry?

He's not going to ask if you got promoted at work – He's going to ask who you promoted in life?

He's not going to ask what kind of house did you live in – He's going to ask did you love your neighbors?

He's not going to ask how much money you made – He's going to ask how much money you gave?

He's not going to ask how much you

OUR FIRST PRIORITY

saved – He's going to ask how many you saved?

Erwin W. Lutzer
"Christianity demands a level of caring that transcends human inclinations."

I'm afraid all too often we are like the sign seen on a church building that said, "We Care About You. Sundays 10 a.m. Only"

A fifteen-year-old boy came bounding into the house and found his mom in bed. He asked if she was sick or something. He was truly concerned. Mom replied that, as a matter of fact, she didn't feel too well. The son replied, "Well, don't worry a bit about dinner. I'll be happy to carry you down to the stove."

Christianity demands a level of caring that transcends human inclinations

It's costly to love the world, to care, to have compassion.

2 Corinthians 12:15
"I will be glad to spend all I have and myself as well in order to help you " (GNB)

The Compassion To Deliver Nations

A.W. Tozer

"Among the plastic saints of our times Jesus has to do all the dying and all we want is to hear another sermon about His dying."

Colossians 3:12
"Therefore, as God's chosen people, holy and dearly loved, clothe yourselves with compassion." (NIV)

Hebrews 10:34
"For you had compassion on me in my chains, and joyfully accepted the plundering of your goods, knowing that you have a better and an enduring possession for yourselves in heaven."

> *If we care, we won't mind a little plundering of our goods for the unloved, the unreached, and the untold.*

If we care we don't mind a little plundering of our goods for the unloved, the unreached, and the untold.

Pablo Casals the Spanish

OUR FIRST PRIORITY

cellist, conductor, and composer said,
"I feel the capacity to care is the thing which gives life its deepest significance."

Pharaoh's daughter didn't know she was delivering a nation, she was just having compassion on a lost child. Your compassion today will make a difference for someone.
Compassion is costly.
Lack of compassion is even more costly.
Compassion moves us.

Paul Brand, M.D
"The body poorly protects what it does not feel. In the spiritual body, also, loss of feeling inevitably leads to atrophy and inner deterioration. So much of the sorrow in the world is due to the selfishness of one living organism that simply does not care when another suffers."

God cares for you and me.
And He wants to use you and me as instruments of His care for those less fortunate.
Compassion is the force that will move us.

CHAPTER SEVEN
THE FATHER'S HEART

The Father's Heart

Luke 15:11-32

"Then He [Jesus] said, 'A certain man had two sons. And the younger of them said to his father, 'Father, give me the portion of goods that falls to me.' So he divided to them his livelihood. And not many days after, the younger son gathered all together, journeyed to a far country, and there wasted his possessions with prodigal living.

"But when he had spent all, there arose a severe famine in that land, and he began to be in want. Then he went and joined himself to a citizen of that country, and he sent him into his fields to feed swine. And he would gladly have filled his stomach with the pods that the swine ate, and no one gave him anything. But when he came to himself, he said, 'How many of my father's hired servants have bread enough and to spare, and I perish with hunger! I will arise and go to my father, and will say to him, Father, I have sinned against heaven and before you, and I am no longer worthy to be called your son. Make me like one of your hired servants.'

"And he arose and came to his father. But when he was still a great way off, his father saw him and had compassion, and ran and fell on his neck and kissed him. And the son said to him, 'Father, I have sinned against heaven and in your sight, and am no longer worthy to be called your son.' But the father said to his servants, 'Bring out the best robe and put it on him, and put a ring on his hand and sandals on his feet. And bring the fatted calf here and kill it, and let us eat and be merry; for this my son was dead and is alive again; he was lost and is found.' And they began to be merry.

"Now his older son was in the field. And as he came and drew near to the house, he heard music and dancing. So he called one of the servants and asked what these things meant. And he said to him, 'Your brother has come, and because he has received him safe and sound, your father has killed the fatted calf.' But he was angry and would not go in. Therefore his father came out and pleaded with him. So he answered and said to his father, 'Lo, these many years I have been serving you; I never transgressed your commandment at any time; and yet you never gave me a young goat, that I might make merry with my friends. But as soon as this son of yours came, who has devoured your livelihood with harlots, you killed the fatted calf for him.'

"And he said to him, 'Son, you are always with me, and all that I have is yours. It was right that we should make merry and be glad, for your brother was dead and is alive again, and was lost and is found.'"

There are two prodigal sons in this story. The first is about the prodigal who was outside the father's house, in another nation, wasting away and in want and destitution.

> *There are two prodigal sons in this story.*

The second is about the elder brother who is the prodigal inside the father's house. The grief he causes the father is even greater than the grief of the first son.

The reason the elder prodigal causes the father such grief is that he is a son in the house, with access to all the father's provision but without the father's vision.

What a grief to the father that his children would flourish in his wonderful provision but be

OUR FIRST PRIORITY

> *It is a grief to the father that his children would flourish in his wonderful provision but be destitute of his passionate vision.*

destitute of his passionate vision.

How much of the Church today has the Father's provision without the Father's vision?

Luke 15:20 says, "But when he was still a great way off, his father saw him and had compassion, and ran and fell on his neck and kissed him."

The father was looking, his eyes were searching. He saw that destitute, barefoot, starving frail frame wrapped in rags while he was still a great way off.

Matthew Henry's Commentary says,
"Here were eyes of mercy, and those eyes quick-sighted: When he was yet a great way off his father saw him, before any other of the family were aware of him, as if from the top of some high tower he had been looking that way which his son had gone..."

The Father's Heart

The elder brother had his father's farm and his field but he did not have his father's eyes.

He had his father's provision but he did not have his father's vision. His focus was far from what his father's focus was.

Do we see what the Father sees? As his sons and daughters do we see what really matters, what's close and dear to His heart? Do you and I have the Father's eyes?

Helen Keller, (born deaf and blind) was asked, "What is the greatest calamity?" She answered, *"To have eyes and not see."*

Matthew 13:15
"For the hearts of this people have grown dull. Their ears are hard of hearing, and their eyes they have closed, lest they should see with their eyes and hear with their ears, lest they should understand with their hearts and turn, so that I should heal them."

Mark 8:18 (Jesus to His disciples)
"Having eyes, do you not see? And having ears, do you not hear? And do you not remember?" It's possible to belong to the Father and not see

OUR FIRST PRIORITY

what He sees. So what does He see? What does He want us to see?

John 4:35
"Do you not say, 'There are still four months [plenty of time] and then comes the harvest'? Behold, I say to you, lift up your eyes and look at the fields, for they are already white for harvest!"

The Father wants us to look at the fields!

He is desperate for us to have a vision for the harvest, for us to see multitudes and multitudes in the valley of decision.

He wants our vision to be focused, looking for those outside the Father's house. He saw that boy while he was a far way off.

If we would have the Father's vision we will be looking for those not just near by but a far way off.

Oswald Chambers said,
"When the Spirit of God comes into a man, He gives him a world-wide view."

The Father's Heart

Matthew 9:36-38

"But when He saw the multitudes, He was moved with compassion for them, because they were weary and scattered, like sheep having no shepherd. Then He said to His disciples, 'The harvest truly is plentiful, but the laborers are few. Therefore pray the Lord of the harvest to send out laborers into His harvest.'"

The Father has such a vision for the harvest. What He sees moves Him.

The elder brother had no vision for those outside the father's house, no vision for the harvest, no dream or desire for the doomed, the damned, and the dying.

> *The elder brother had no vision for those outside the father's house.*

Luke 15:20 says, "But when he was still a great way off, his father saw him and had compassion, and ran and fell on his neck and kissed him."

This verse teaches us five things about the Father:

OUR FIRST PRIORITY

1. The Father has Eyes of Mercy.

What He sees moves Him with mercy and pity and kindness. When He looks at the least, the last, and the lost, He loves them and longs for them.

2. The Father has a Heart of Mercy.

There was a yearning in him at the sight of his son.

He had compassion on him. This boy had brought all his sorrow on himself. But all the father could do was to reach out to him with a tender forgiving, merciful heart.

Hosea 11:8
"How can I give you up, Ephraim? How can I hand you over, Israel? How can I make you like Admah? How can I set you like Zeboiim? My heart churns within Me; my sympathy is stirred."

We don't see this stirring in the elder brother. He had the father's house, but he did

The Father's Heart

> *The elder brother had the father's house, but he did not have the father's heart.*

not have the father's heart.

3. The Father has Feet of Mercy.

He saw him, he had compassion on him, and he ran to him. The father's feet are fast to furnish his forgiveness.

There is urgency in the Father. Time is critical to the ones outside of God's house. Eternity is only one heartbeat away from every perishing man and woman. Fifty-one million people die and enter eternity every year. A million people a week. One hundred and forty-three thousand people will enter eternity today. Thirty-five thousand will have died today and never once heard the name of Jesus.

The father ran. He did not want another moment to pass for the prodigal outside of his mercy and forgiveness. Our Father knows and understands the critical condition and the desperate dilemma of the lost.

There was no sense of this urgency in the

elder brother. He had the father's fortune but he did not have the father's feet.

4. The Father has Arms of Mercy.

His arms stretched out to embrace him: He fell on his son's neck. Though the son is guilty and filthy and reeking with the stench from feeding swine, the father takes him in his arms, and lays him in his bosom.

Psalm 136:12
"With a strong hand, and with an outstretched arm…His mercy endures forever."

Isaiah 1:18
"Come now, and let us reason together," says the LORD, "Though your sins are like scarlet, they shall be as white as snow; though they are red like crimson, they shall be as wool."

We don't see the elder brother reaching out with the father's arms. He had the father's estate but he did not have the father's estimate of a lost life.

The Father's Heart

He had the father's assets but he did not have the father's assessment of what a soul is truly worth.

He had the father's valuables but he did not have the father's valuation of a person perishing outside the father's house.

Do you and I have the Father's arms today? Or are our arms too full, carrying all the wonderful provision of the Father? Arms abounding with blessing but too full to bear His burden? Are they too full to lift the load of getting the Gospel to the least, the last, and the lost?

> *The elder brother was blessed with the father's blessing but he was not burdened with the father's burden.*

The elder brother was blessed with the father's blessing but was not burdened with the father's burden.

The Apostle Paul did not have this problem.

He said (Romans 9:1-3)
"I tell the truth in Christ, I am not lying, my conscience also bearing me witness in the Holy

OUR FIRST PRIORITY

Spirit, that I have great sorrow and continual grief in my heart. For I could wish that I myself were accursed from Christ for my brethren, my countrymen according to the flesh."

Paul, unlike the elder brother, bore the Father's burden for perishing people. He valued what God valued.

His estimate of the lost was higher than his estimate of himself. The value he placed on perishing people was greater than the value he placed on his own life.

> *The value Paul placed on perishing people was greater than the value he placed on his own life.*

That was the value Jesus placed on you and me. He gave up His life for us all.

The father has eyes of mercy, he saw him far off.

The father has a heart of mercy, he had compassion.

The father has feet of mercy, he ran to him.

The father has arms of mercy, he embraced him.

5. The Father has Lips of Mercy.

Luke 15:20
"But when he was still a great way off, his father saw him and had compassion, and ran and fell on his neck and kissed him."

Matthew Henry says, *"Here were lips of mercy, and those lips dripping as a honey-comb: He kissed him. This kiss not only assured him of his welcome, but sealed his pardon, his former follies all forgiven."*

The father's lips do not mention his foolishness against him, not one word is said by way of condemnation. The father's lips kiss him and pardon him and welcome him and absolve him.

The elder brother has the father's lands that flow with milk and honey but not the father's lips that flow with grace and mercy.

Listen to him:

Luke 15:30
"But as soon as this son of yours came, who has

devoured your livelihood with harlots, you killed the fatted calf for him."

The elder brother had the father's prosperity but he did not have the father's priority!

Look at the elder brother's priority:

Luke 15:29
"So he answered and said to his father, 'Lo, these many years I have been serving you; I never transgressed your commandment at any time; and yet you never gave me a young goat, that I might make merry with my friends.'"

> *The elder brother had the father's prosperity but he did not have the father's priority!*

What a small priority!

Look at the Father's priority:

Mark 16:15
"And He said to them, 'Go into all the world and preach the Gospel to every creature.'"

According to John 3:16, the Father's priority

The Father's Heart

is that none should perish. What is your priority today? What is your attitude toward those outside the Father's house?

Do you have the Father's salvation, and healing and forgiveness and prosperity and mercy and love? Do you have the Father's goods without the Father's goals? Do you have the Father's possessions without the Father's purposes? Do you have the Father's objects without the Father's objectives?

What if the elder brother had become a partner with the father? What if he not only had the father's provision but also shared the father's vision?

What if he had been looking with the father and saw with him the prodigal while he was still a long way off?

What a joy he could have been to his father. He could have ran with him and reached out with him and partnered with him in welcoming the prodigal home.

What would it have meant to the father to know that his son not only had his possessions but also his purposes?

How different this story would be if the

OUR FIRST PRIORITY

father found out that his elder son not only had his provision but also his vision.

Oh, that the elder brother would have eyes of mercy and a heart of mercy and feet of mercy and arms of mercy and lips of mercy.

What if his focus was off of himself and on those outside the father's house? What a team he could have been with the father!

1 Corinthians 3:9
"For we are God's fellow workers..."

1 Corinthians 3:9
"For we are laborers together with God..." (KJV)

The Father is calling us to work with Him, to partner with Him, to become His accomplices and associates in harvesting the earth!

Luke 10:2
"Then He said to them, 'The harvest truly is great, but the

laborers are few; therefore pray the Lord of the harvest to send out laborers into His harvest.'"

We have so much from the Father. But He wants us to have more than just His provision; He wants us to have His vision.

He has given us His prosperity to perform His priority.

We have been given His possessions and provision that we may partner with His passion and purpose.

Which son are you today? The one that is away from the Father's house, wasting your life with empty living - or the one that lives in the Father's house but does not have His heart for perishing people?

Or maybe you're the son that has the Father's provision as well as the Father's vision. The son or daughter that delights the Father, that partners with Him in His plan and purpose for a lost and dying world.

The first son wasted his possessions with prodigal living. The elder son wasted his possessions with purposeless living.

But there is another son who uses his

OUR FIRST PRIORITY

possessions for priority living. He or she lives to make Jesus' last command their *first priority*.

Prodigal living - Living outside the Father's house.
Purposeless living - Living inside the Father's house but outside of His vision.
Priority living - Living inside the Father's house and for the Father's vision. Where the Father's provision is utilized for the Father's vision.

This is what we are called to.

CHAPTER EIGHT
LET'S GO TO THE OTHER SIDE

Let's Go To The Other Side

Luke 8:22

"Now it happened, on a certain day, that He got into a boat with His disciples. And He said to them, 'Let us cross over to the other side of the lake.' And they launched out."

Jesus was, and is, a man of vision, direction and purpose. He was born for, lived for, and died for a cause. He lived the most focused life ever lived!

There was purpose in His majestic heart on this particular day when He said to His disciples, "Let's cross over to the other side of the lake." Jesus knew that on the 'other side' of the water there was a tormented, terrified man who had been afflicted by a legion of devils.

This poor man was driven, deranged, and destitute. He roamed the tombs like a wild animal. He was unclothed, uncouth, and unclean.

He had been shackled and bound with chains many times but with frenzied fury and satanic strength he would snap the chains asunder.

This man was a terror to himself and to all

who saw him.

Jesus knew what was on the other side and He knew who was on the other side. Jesus is the life liberator. He's the restorer, the repairer of the breach - the hope and help of humanity.

> *Jesus is the life liberator. He's the restorer, the repairer of the breach - the hope and help of humanity.*

John 10:10
"The thief does not come except to steal, and to kill, and to destroy. I have come that they may have life, and that they may have it more abundantly."

1 John 3:8
"…For this purpose the Son of God was manifested, that He might destroy the works of the devil."

Wherever you find hurting, helpless and hopeless people you will find a loving Savior calling out to His disciples, "Let's go over to the other side."

And so they launched out. They committed.

Let's Go To The Other Side

They faith promised. They got in the boat. It was a great day. The sun was shining, the sails were shimmering and the Savior was smiling.

There was exuberance, excitement and emotion. The smell of adventure was permeating the air. A sense of destiny descended on the disciples.

"Yes!" They felt like Nehemiah when he boldly proclaimed, "I'm doing a great work!"

They were going from the mundane of fishermen to the mandate of fishers of men!

Jesus the captain was leading the crew. The commander had spoken. The mission had been ordered. The vision was set before them.

> *They were going from the mundane of fishermen to the mandate of fishers of men!*

The church had responded. The disciples were in the boat heading to the other side!

This is the command of Jesus to us this very day.

Mark 16:15
"He said to them, 'Go into all the world and preach the good news to all creation.'" (NIV)

OUR FIRST PRIORITY

The other side must hear the good news. All the families of the earth must have an opportunity to go to heaven.

Matthew 28:19-20
"Therefore go and make disciples of all nations, baptizing them in the name of the Father and of the Son and of the Holy Spirit, and teaching them to obey everything I have commanded you. And surely I am with you always, to the very end of the age." (NIV)

We also have His charge and command to go to the other side. As long as there are lost people, people without the Gospel, people without the opportunity to believe in Jesus, His clarion call is still ringing out; *to the other side!*

And there is nothing more exciting and fulfilling than launching out in obedience to His mission. What is more exhilarating than getting in the boat with Jesus for the cause of reaching those on the other side?

This is what we were made for. This is why He has a Church on the earth and disciples on the planet.

We were made for a mission.
We were created for a cause.
We were designed for a destiny.

So they launched out, full of faith and vision brimming with a sense of significance.

Luke 8:23
"But as they sailed He fell asleep. And a windstorm came down on the lake, and they were filling with water, and were in jeopardy."

It's a lot easier to start out than it is to finish up. It's a lot easier to make a faith promise than it is to give month after month.

While the sun is shining it's fairly easy to get in the boat but when the storm's raging it's not so easy to stay in the boat. When Jesus seems near our faith is high but when He seems to be sleeping and the storm is raging, our faith is not so high.

We know that it was the devil that caused this storm because Jesus rebuked it. There is a real enemy who desperately wants to silence our message. He wants to divert, deflect, distract and

OUR FIRST PRIORITY

detour our mission.

> *There is a real enemy who desperately wants to silence our message. He wants to divert, deflect, distract and detour our mission.*

He knows we are on a faith journey. So he will get the waves as high as he can, to get our faith as low as he can.

"Quit believing! Quit sacrificing! Quit giving! Quit standing in faith! Quit sending friends and funds to the mission field! You can't afford it!"

What do we do when the clouds of doubt and the storms of disbelief beat against us, and beat against our finances and our faith promises and try to keep us from making it to the other side?

I believe we must see that there are two sets of clouds.

The first is the dark clouds of the enemy sent to scare us and to discourage and stop us. But the second is the great cloud of witnesses spoken of in Hebrews that beckon us and encourage us and inspire us to keep going.

Let's Go To The Other Side

Hebrews 12:1

"Therefore we also, since we are surrounded by so great a cloud of witnesses, let us lay aside every weight, and the sin which so easily ensnares us, and let us run with endurance the race that is set before us."

This is the great cloud of those who have already run their race and who have already endured their storms. They have already overcome the devil and fulfilled their destiny. They've already sealed forever their work for God on the earth.

They are in the grandstands of heaven right now cheering you, applauding you, yelling out to you, barracking for you. It's like what we saw here in Sydney during the Olympics.

They're there in the hall of fame; their names are listed in the hall of faith of Hebrews 11. Look at them there. They are all shouting their encouragement.

Abel is saying, "Don't be afraid to offer your best offerings and sacrifices to God. When you're dead they will continue to speak for you."

OUR FIRST PRIORITY

> *Abel is saying, "Don't be afraid to offer your best offerings and sacrifices to God.*

Enoch is saying, "Walk with God, walk with God, walk with God. Don't waver or give up, keep walking with Him and one day you'll just walk right out of there into His presence."

Noah is saying, "Obey God. Obey Him! Even when you're not sure what's happening or going on. If He tells you to do something – do it! Obeying God is how you save yourself."

Abraham is saying, "Go where He tells you to go. Remember the earth is not your home, you're just a pilgrim and a sojourner looking for a city with foundations whose maker and builder is God. Don't get too attached to the temporal dwellings of the earth, it's not your home!"

Moses is saying, "The purposes of Christ are of greater value than the treasures of Egypt. I forsook Egypt for the treasures of Christ and I'm eternally grateful I did!"

When the enemy brings his storm clouds to stop us from going to the other side, let's look a little higher at the other set of clouds, the great cloud of witnesses cheering us on.

Luke 8:24
"And they came to Him and awoke Him, saying, 'Master, Master, we are perishing!' Then He arose and rebuked the wind and the raging of the water. And they ceased, and there was a calm."

When we've left the shore – when we've stepped out in commitment, when we're sailing in deep waters based on the Word we got back on the shore – and the storm arises and water starts filling the boat and we're afraid - we need to wake up the Word of God in our heart.

Jesus is the Word of God.

John 1:1
"In the beginning was the Word, and the Word was with God, and the Word was God." (NIV)

We've got to stir ourselves, remind ourselves of the Word. Wake it up! Don't doubt in the dark what God gave you in the light.

OUR FIRST PRIORITY

2 Peter 3:1-3

"Beloved, I now write to you this second epistle (in both of which I stir up your pure minds by way of reminder), that you may be mindful of the words which were spoken before by the holy prophets, and of the commandment of us, the apostles of the Lord and Savior."

Wake up the Word! The minute we forget the Word we become fearful and self-focused.

Listen to the disciples' focus, "Master we are perishing!" Mark's version says, "Don't you care that we are perishing?"

It's so easy to lose focus when we lose sight of the vision. It's so easy to only see our needs and not the needs of those to whom we are sent.

They weren't perishing; they were just in a storm. The man on the 'other side' however, was the one perishing. It's just like the devil to get my eyes off the people who are perishing and onto my temporary problem.

All of my problems are temporary. But those on the 'other side' of salvation have eternal problems.

Let's Go To The Other Side

Luke 8:25

"But He said to them, 'Where is your faith?' And they were afraid, and marveled, saying to one another, 'Who can this be? For He commands even the winds and water, and they obey Him!'"

Jesus wasn't very sympathetic to the disciples. Instead of, "Oh poor babies, big bad storm and water in the boat...!" – it was, "I said we must go to the other side, where is your faith?"

> *Jesus wasn't very sympathetic to the disciples.*

It takes faith to reach the man on the other side. His situation is so desperate and we are his only hope. In our boat is the power of the Word that will set him free. We must reach him.

Our missions commitment is not a pleasure cruise or a sailing tour. It is a desperate mission of mercy. It's not a casual day out at the lake where we just do what we can, but a desperate journey of dire consequences.

OUR FIRST PRIORITY

> *It takes faith to reach the man on the other side. His situation is so desperate and we are his only hope.*

Luke 8:26-39

"Then they sailed to the country of the Gadarenes, which is opposite Galilee. And when He stepped out on the land, there met Him a certain man from the city who had demons for a long time. And he wore no clothes, nor did he live in a house but in the tombs. When he saw Jesus, he cried out, fell down before Him, and with a loud voice said, 'What have I to do with You, Jesus, Son of the Most High God? I beg You, do not torment me!' For He had commanded the unclean spirit to come out of the man. For it had often seized him, and he was kept under guard, bound with chains and shackles; and he broke the bonds and was driven by the demon into the wilderness.

"Jesus asked him, saying, 'What is your name?' And he said, 'Legion,' because many demons had entered him. And they begged Him that He would not command them to go out into the abyss. Now a herd of many swine was feeding there on the mountain. And they begged Him that He would permit them to enter them. And He permitted them. Then the demons went out of the man and entered the swine, and the herd ran violently down the steep place into the lake and drowned.

"When those who fed them saw what had happened, they fled and told it in the city and in the country. Then they went out to see what had happened, and came to Jesus, and found the man from whom the demons had departed, sitting at the feet of Jesus, clothed and in his right mind. And they were afraid. They also who had seen it told them by what means he who had been demon-possessed was healed.

"Then the whole multitude of the surrounding region of the Gadarenes asked Him to depart from them, for they were seized with great fear. And He got into the boat and returned.

"Now the man from whom the demons had departed begged Him that he might be with Him. But Jesus sent him away, saying, 'Return to your own house, and tell what great things

OUR FIRST PRIORITY

God has done for you.' And he went his way and proclaimed throughout the whole city what great things Jesus had done for him."

In the Gospel of Mark it says he went and preached Jesus in the 10 cities around the region. How important was it that they went to the other side?

How many lives this very day depend on what you and I do?

The great cloud of witnesses are cheering us on. The enemy is trying to stir up new storms to keep us from the other side. Those on the other side are more desperate than ever.

Jesus is saying to those of us who have stepped out into the boat, "Where is your faith? Use your faith, go to the other side."

You and I are the key players in the plan of God for the earth.

You weren't called to sit on the side of the shore and watch. You are called to get the Word to the other side.

CHAPTER NINE
THAT NONE SHOULD PERISH

That None Should Perish

John 3:16
"For God so loved the world that He gave His only begotten Son, that whoever believes in Him should not perish but have everlasting life."

Martin Luther said these 25 words of John 3:16 are the whole Bible in a nutshell. He called them the condensed Bible.

In this one verse of Scripture we see the who, the what, and the why of the Bible.

WHO? – God…God who loved the world so much.

John 17:23
"… and that the world may know that You have sent Me, and have loved them as You have loved Me."

> *God loves you and me and the whole world as much as He loves Jesus.*

God loves you and me and the whole world as much as He loves Jesus.

I was in prayer about eight years ago out in Wallacia, NSW, where we lived in a lovely house that we rented. One day Carol had gone shopping and the kids were in school. I decided I was going to spend that morning in prayer. That's not a bad thing for a pastor or a Christian to do. I'll never forget that day as long as I live. During my time of prayer I totally laid myself on the floor in the lounge room. And I began to just look at God, meditating and contemplating on Him. I said, *"Father I have not come this morning to ask you for anything, I've just come here to lay here in front of you and gaze upon you and to love, adore and to worship you. I've committed this season this morning to be with you intimately, the house is clear, everyone's gone, and I'm just going to lay here for a while Lord. I'm going to lift my soul up to you in adoration."*

It was a wonderful time. Normally, I would not share this time with you because it was very private, however what happened that day I do feel I need to share. All of a sudden, in the midst of this season of prayer and adoration, looking to God, I saw a vision. It was very clear. I saw something that I could not believe I was seeing. And I wasn't making it up, because every scene of it was surprising me and taking my breath away. In this vision, I saw a scene in heaven. It was a scene of God the Father gazing and looking upon His Son. And the light of His Son was in His face: God was delighting in His Son. Jesus is the delight of God. Jesus is the joy of God. God is so pleased with Jesus. God loves Jesus, God delights in Jesus. Everything Jesus is, God delights in. I was actually watching the Father delight in His Son. I could see it in the Father's eyes. I'm a father. I know what I saw. And the gaze of the Father was on Him and I witnessed the delight, the joy that was coming to the Father by just gazing upon His Son. I watched that scene. I didn't even think I should be looking at a scene like that. I thought it was too intimate.

And then in a moment I saw the Son rise up and walk out of the Father's presence. And it was as though He had walked out of a film, I could see the perforated holes of a roll of film. The scene changed. Jesus literally walked from that motion picture film, to another complete scene that was an incredible contrast. In this scene, all of a sudden, Jesus who was the delight of the Father, was on the cross, stripped,

OUR FIRST PRIORITY

bleeding, naked, carrying the sin of the world, totally despised. Everything God hated, Jesus had become on the cross. Everything God loathes, everything God punishes, Jesus became on the cross. He became what 2 Corinthians 5:21 calls, sin. He became sin.

The contrast was so amazing. And now, He who had been the delight of the Father was the despised of the Father. He who was everything the Father loved, was now everything the Father hated.

And this contrast was taking my breath away. The Father then turned His back, hating everything the Son had now become, because the Son took on that which was sinful, wicked, proud, selfish, racist, arrogant and immoral. He became sin on the cross. And my head was spinning.

> *He who was everything the Father loved, was now everything the Father hated.*

Then a moment later, the scene changed again.

Jesus now walked right back into that very scene from the beginning. He walked through the corner of that film and back to the very place where He had been before, but now He was scarred. Jesus sat down across from the Father again. And I looked and watched the Father gaze upon His Son with such delight, such joy. I saw again the joy that the Father had in His Son. Oh, the delight that the Son was to the Father. But there was a major difference now. This scene was totally different from the first scene, because now I was sitting next to Jesus. Jesus brought me with Him to the Father. And now the Father was looking at *me* the same way He was looking at Jesus. What love; that Jesus would go to rebellious humanity, wicked humanity, blaspheming humanity and bring us back to the Father.

Romans 5:6-8
"For when we were still without strength, in due time Christ died for the ungodly. For scarcely for a righteous man will one die; yet perhaps for a good man someone would even dare to die. But God demonstrates His own love toward us, in that while we were still sinners, Christ died for us."

OUR FIRST PRIORITY

What extravagant love!
What beyond measure abandonment for others!
What excessive commitment to our well being!
What total self-sacrifice for sin filled strangers!

Ephesians 2:4-7
"But God, who is rich in mercy, because of His great love with which He loved us, even when we were dead in trespasses, made us alive together with Christ (by grace you have been saved), and raised us up together, and made us sit together in the heavenly places in Christ Jesus, that in the ages to come He might show the exceeding riches of His grace in His kindness toward us in Christ Jesus."

THIS IS THE GREATEST LOVE IN THE UNIVERSE!

John 15:13
"Greater love has no one than this, than to lay down one's life for his friends."

WHO? Who is the Bible all about? It's all about God, who loved the world so much.

WHAT? That He gave His only begotten Son.

Jesus is God's gift to you and I. God bankrupt heaven for you and I, to give us the free gift of His Son.

> *God bankrupt heaven to send Jesus to the earth.*

John 4:10
"Jesus answered and said to her, 'If you knew the gift of God, and who it is who says to you, 'Give Me a drink,' you would have asked Him, and He would have given you living water.'"

Romans 6:23
"For the wages of sin is death, but the gift of God is eternal life in Christ Jesus our Lord."

Romans 8:32
"He who did not spare His own Son, but delivered Him up for us all, how shall He not with Him also freely give us all things?"

What God did was to give us the gift of His Son. What God did for us is inexpressible.

OUR FIRST PRIORITY

What God did for us is inconceivable.
What God did for us is beyond belief.

2 Corinthians 9:15
"Thanks be to God for His indescribable gift!"

WHO? God – 1 John 4:8 says God is love.
WHAT? He gave His only Begotten Son.
WHY? This is the big question.

My kids have always seemed to love this question. "Why daddy?"

When they were little I would say, "Because I'm the papa! Because I'm big and you're little! Because I said so, that's why." I noticed that when they got older those explanations didn't seem to work quite as well. I had to come up with better reasons.

> *The why is always the mission statement of the person or the organization.*

'Why' is the important question. The why of a thing always gives us the purpose and the reason. The why is always the 'mission statement' of any person or organization.

For example, Disneyland's vision statement is, 'To make people happy.' That's why they exist. Everything they do, every dollar they spend, every staff member they hire, every new attraction they design is to make people happy. Everybody who goes to work at Disneyland knows why they are there.

Every major company or organization worth its salt has a mission statement; a why. It would be terrible to go to work for somebody and not know why you are there or why they are there.

I believe the God of the universe has a why. I believe we cannot only know who and what, but we see clearly in John 3:16 God's mission statement... the why.

The mission statement of the whole Bible, the plan and purpose of God – "that whosoever believes in Him should not perish but have everlasting life."

God's mission statement in four words:
THAT NONE SHOULD PERISH.

The whole plan and purpose of God is that none would perish. No one. Not one man or

OUR FIRST PRIORITY

> *The whole plan and purpose of God is that none would perish. Not one. Not one man or woman or boy or girl.*

woman or boy or girl. God's will and passion and purpose is that nobody perish but that everybody has eternal life.

This is God's mission. Motivated by His love. Procured by the giving of His Son to die for our sins. In order, that none should perish.

John 10:27-28
"My sheep hear My voice, and I know them, and they follow Me. And I give them eternal life, and they shall never perish; neither shall anyone snatch them out of My hand."

2 Peter 3:9
"The Lord is not slack concerning His promise, as some count slackness, but is longsuffering toward us, not willing that any should perish but that all should come to repentance."

God's mission and passion is that none should perish.

But unless men and women repent and believe the Gospel, they WILL perish.

Luke 13:1-5
"There were present at that season some who told Him about the Galileans whose blood Pilate had mingled with their sacrifices. And Jesus answered and said to them, 'Do you suppose that these Galileans were worse sinners than all other Galileans, because they suffered such things? I tell you, no; but unless you repent you will all likewise perish. Or those 18 on whom the tower in Siloam fell and killed them, do you think that they were worse sinners than all other men who dwelt in Jerusalem? I tell you, no; but unless you repent you will all likewise perish.'"

God sent and sacrificed Jesus that none should perish. And now you and I who have been born again have been called to His side for this purpose. Jesus has now called you and me to be part of His mission.

John 20:21
"So Jesus said to them again, 'Peace to you!

OUR FIRST PRIORITY

As the Father has sent Me, I also send you.'"

There are a lot of Christians today who would say, "Wait a minute. I'm not an evangelist. This doesn't give me peace! I'm shy, I'm quiet, I'm reserved, I'm not an extrovert, I'm just the opposite!"

And yet Jesus said you are just as sent as He was. You are as much on this mission as He is. Let me tell you how you get peace, by obeying Jesus! If you are a shy person then go find all the shy people you can and relate to them in your shyness and tell them about Jesus. Just say to them, "You're shy and I'm shy, you're quiet and I'm quiet, I can relate to you and in my relating to you let me tell you about Jesus."

> *Jesus said you are just as sent as He was. You are as much on this mission as He is.*

Mark 16:15-16
"And He said to them, 'Go into all the world and preach the Gospel to every creature. He who believes and is baptized will be saved; but he who does

not believe will be condemned.'"

This is the default call of God on every Christian.

This is called the Great Commission. CO-MISSION. It means common mission; it means the cause and purpose we share in common with God. This mission that none should perish. God has called you and I to His Mission and it is not optional. People perishing without the Gospel is not an option!

2 Corinthians 5:15
"...and He died for all, that those who live should live no longer for themselves, but for Him who died for them and rose again."

We are not to live unto ourselves but unto Him who died for us. We are now as Christians called to serve not our own agenda but God's mission.

1 Corinthians 10:24
"Let no one seek his own, but each one the other's well-being."

OUR FIRST PRIORITY

2 Timothy 2:3-4
"You therefore must endure hardship as a good soldier of Jesus Christ. No one engaged in warfare entangles himself with the affairs of this life, that he may please him who enlisted him as a soldier."

Now I know that these are not very popular Scriptures. But they are nonetheless the core and crux of Christianity.

Most of us in the western world have such a self-focused Christianity. So much of our western version of Christianity is focused on 'me and now'. Me and now. "What's in it for me?" and "I want it right now." "What's God got for me, and whatever it is I want it now."

> *We have not been saved for ourselves we've been saved FROM ourselves!*

Contrast this with the rest of the world, those in developing countries who love Jesus with all their hearts; their focus is not on me and now, but on others and eternity.

We have not been saved for ourselves – we've been

saved FROM ourselves!

We've been saved for Him. For His plans and His purpose.

Some today are asking, "What's God's plan for my life?" When people ask me to pray for them concerning God's plan for their life I decline. I won't pray that prayer. It is the wrong prayer. The question is not, "What's God's plan for my life?" The question should be, "What's God's plan?" Once you know His plan you don't have to be a rocket scientist to figure out what you are supposed to do with your life. Just get your life wrapped around His plan and you will be pretty close to having His plan for your life.

> *The question is not "What's God's plan for my life?" The question should be, "What's God's plan?"*

God's plan is that no one perish. Get your life wrapped around that and I guarantee you, you will have His plan for your life. It's not about your life. It's about His plan.

His plan: That none should perish.

We don't have to be real

OUR FIRST PRIORITY

brilliant to figure out what were supposed to do with our life when we understand His plan.

So many of us are like Jonah. We are called, equipped, gifted, but wrong *focused*.

You see Nineveh was doomed. But God so wanted to show mercy. Their only hope was to repent. But God knew they would never repent without a messenger. So He called Jonah, He equipped him and commissioned him.

But Jonah went the other way. Jonah's focus was not perishing cities. His focus was on something else. Look at his focus.

Jonah 1:17-2:1-10
"Now the LORD had prepared a great fish to swallow Jonah. And Jonah was in the belly of the fish three days and three nights. Then Jonah prayed to the LORD his God from the fish's belly. And he said: 'I cried out to the LORD because of my affliction, and He answered me. Out of the belly of Sheol I cried, and You heard my voice. For You cast me into the deep, into the heart of the seas, and the floods surrounded me; all Your billows and Your waves passed over me.

"Then I said, 'I have been cast out of Your sight; yet I will look again toward Your holy temple.' The waters surrounded me, even to my soul; the deep closed around me; weeds were wrapped around my head. I went down to the moorings of the mountains; the earth with its bars closed behind me forever; yet You have brought up my life from the pit, O LORD, my God. When my soul fainted within me, I remembered the LORD; and my prayer went up to You, into Your holy temple. Those who regard worthless idols forsake their own mercy. But I will sacrifice to You with the voice of thanksgiving; I will pay what I have vowed. Salvation is of the LORD.' So the LORD spoke to the fish, and it vomited Jonah onto dry land."

In this passage we get a good look at Jonah's focus:

"I cried; my affliction; He answered me; my voice; me into the deep; surrounded me, passed over me; I said; I have been cast out; I will look; surrounded me; around me, my head; I went, behind me; my life; my soul; within me; I remembered; my prayer; I will; I will."

OUR FIRST PRIORITY

No wonder the fish vomited him out!

That kind of self-focus would make any self-respecting fish sick. Now here was the deal - Nineveh was perishing! How would you like to be perishing and have your salvation committed to someone like Jonah?!

Well the truth is, friend, that someone *is* perishing and his or her salvation *is* dependent on your commitment to God's mission.

While you and I are flourishing, the world is perishing.

God has co-missioned you and I in order that none should perish.

> *While you and I are flourishing, the world is perishing.*

2 Corinthians 5:18-20
"All this is from God, who reconciled us to himself through Christ and gave us the ministry of reconciliation: that God was reconciling the world to Himself in Christ, not counting men's sins against them. And he has committed to us the message of reconciliation. We are therefore Christ's ambassadors, as though God were making his appeal through us.

We implore you on Christ's behalf: be reconciled to God." (NIV)

What will you DO that none should perish?
What will you SAY that none should perish?
What will you GIVE that none should perish?
How will you CHANGE YOUR FOCUS that none would perish?

WILL YOU CO-MISSION WITH GOD?

Or is your heart like Jonah's – it's enough that you're saved, it's enough that you're blessed, it's enough that you're not perishing.

I remember years ago as a high school student going to hear a preacher that came through my hometown in Arizona. He told a story I will never forget. He said he was driving home one night somewhere in the South with his wife and two daughters in the car. It was raining and dark and because of the intensity of the rain he could hardly see past his headlights. On the way home he had to drive over a huge bridge. There were signs posted all along the bridge that said, "Do not pick up hitchhikers." There was an institute for the criminally insane near the base

OUR FIRST PRIORITY

of the bridge and sometimes people would escape from it and try to hitch a ride. On this particular night, as he turned his car on to the bridge, he had to drive exceptionally slow because he could hardly see the road. Somewhere near the top of the bridge a man suddenly appeared in the headlights. He was soaked, standing in the middle of the road with his shirt off frantically waving it over his head, his eyes as wide as Buick hubcaps screaming like a banshee. This preacher's wife began to say, "Oh please don't stop, try to drive around him!" But the man was unavoidable and there was nowhere for the car to go to miss him. So he had to stop the car and as soon as he did the man slapped his hands down on the hood of the car and was screaming at the top of his lungs.

The preacher looked over at his wife and said to lock the door after him and not to unlock it until he returned. His family now was crying and pleading with him to not get out of the car. He opened the door and stepped outside. He was immediately soaked from the rain. As he approached the front of the car to grab the man all of a sudden he could make out what the man was screaming. "The bridge is out! The bridge is out! A bus load of kids just went over!" As these words registered in the pastor's mind he looked back in the car at his wife and two daughters. He wrapped his arms around the man and wept in gratitude. The preacher stood there with the man for the next half-hour in the middle of the road, waving his jacket above his head screaming, "The bridge is out, the bridge is out!"

For a lost and dying world the bridge is out. For people headed to a Christless eternity the bridge is out. Where are the men and women who will stand in the middle of the road and forbid people to perish? In John 3:16 we see the who, the what and the why of the Bible. The Bible is about God who loves the world so much. The Bible is about Jesus, God's gift to the world. The Bible is about the mission and passion of God, that none should perish.

> *Where are the men and women who will stand in the road and forbid people to perish?*

Jonah was so focused on

OUR FIRST PRIORITY

himself.

Jesus is so focused on others.
Who are you focused on?

CHAPTER TEN
GOD'S PLAN FOR THE AGES

Isaiah 42:4

"He will not fail nor be discouraged, till He has established justice in the earth; and the coastlands shall wait for His law."

God has a plan. It will not fail because God cannot fail.

Jeremiah 32:17

"Ah, Lord GOD! Behold, You have made the heavens and the earth by Your great power and outstretched arm. There is nothing too hard for You."

> *God has a plan. It will not fail because God cannot fail.*

When God says something is going to happen, it's going to happen. When God decides something and formulates a plan, that plan cannot possibly fail.

Jeremiah 32:27

"Behold, I am the LORD, the God of all flesh. Is there anything too hard for Me?"

OUR FIRST PRIORITY

If every king and dictator and devil and cult and terrorist and religion in the world were to combine all their power and resources against Him, it would be as a joke to God.

Psalm 2:1-12
"What fools the nations are to rage against the Lord! How strange that men should try to outwit God! For a summit conference of the nations has been called to plot against the Lord and his Messiah, Christ the King. 'Come, let us break his chains,' they say, 'and free ourselves from all this slavery to God.' But God in heaven merely laughs! He is amused by all their puny plans. And then in fierce fury he rebukes them and fills them with fear. For the Lord declares, 'This is the King of my choice, and I have enthroned Him in Jerusalem, my holy city.' His chosen one replies, 'I will reveal the everlasting purposes of God, for the Lord has said to me, 'You are my Son. This is your Coronation Day. Today I am giving you your glory.' 'Only ask and I will give you all the nations of the world. Rule them with an iron rod; smash them like clay pots!' O kings and rulers of the earth, listen

while there is time. Serve the Lord with reverent fear; rejoice with trembling. Fall down before his Son and kiss his feet before his anger is roused and you perish. I am warning you - his wrath will soon begin. But oh, the joys of those who put their trust in Him!" (TLB)

Who can stand against Him?
Who can rage against Him?
Who can out think Him?
Who can thwart His plans?

> *God's heart and passion is for the earth to be redeemed and for justice and mercy to reign.*

Job 42:2
"I know that you can do all things; no plan of yours can be thwarted." (NIV)

So what is His plan for the earth? What is His desire for the nations? God's heart and passion is for the earth to be redeemed and for justice and mercy to reign.

There are people today who will live their whole life

on this planet and never know a single day of justice. They live under corrupt regimes of cruelty and ruthlessness. Innocent children have their limbs chopped off or are thrown into fires in acts of unbelievable inhumanity.

Their cry to God is for justice and mercy and redemption. He has a plan. It will not fail.

Habakkuk 2:14
"For the earth will be filled with the knowledge of the glory of the LORD, as the waters cover the sea."

This is His plan and nothing can keep it from happening.

Psalm 22:27
"All the ends of the world shall remember and turn to the LORD, and all the families of the nations shall worship before You."

Psalm 67:1-3
"God be merciful to us and bless us, and cause His face to shine upon us. (Selah)
That Your way may be known on earth, your

salvation among all nations. Let the peoples praise You, O God; let all the peoples praise You."

The Living Bible says it this way,
"O God, in mercy bless us; let your face beam with joy as you look down at us. Send us around the world with the news of your saving power and your eternal plan for all mankind. How everyone throughout the earth will praise the Lord!" (Psalm 67:1-3)

His plan is that the news of His saving power be delivered to the whole earth.

Psalm 72:19
"And blessed be His glorious name forever! And let the whole earth be filled with His glory. Amen and Amen."

You say, but how can this happen? I tell you it's happening right now! It is harvest time all over the earth! The fields of the earth are white unto harvest right now.

Tens of thousands of people are being born

OUR FIRST PRIORITY

again every day – some statistics say as many as a million Chinese a month and a million Latin Americans every 6 weeks! Nearly half of Africa is already converted!

Evangelical Christianity is growing at a rate three to four times faster than the birth rate!

The question is not so much how will this happen but what part will you have in making it happen?

The harvest of the earth, the Gospel to the nations is going to happen. It's already happening. God is not waiting on you and me to die to our materialism and self-focus and our lukewarm commitment to the Great Commission. He's doing it now. Will you do it with Him?

> *God is no longer waiting on you and me to die to our materialism and self-focus and our lukewarm commitment to the Great Commission.*

We have an amazing record in the book of Revelation. The book of Revelation is prophecy written as history. It's what's going to happen written in the past tense.

> *The book of Revelation is prophecy written as history. It's the history of the future!*

It's the history of the future!

Revelation 7:9-10
"After these things I looked, and behold, a great multitude which no one could number, of all nations, tribes, peoples, and tongues, standing before the throne and before the Lamb, clothed with white robes, with palm branches in their hands, and crying out with a loud voice, saying, 'Salvation belongs to our God who sits on the throne, and to the Lamb!'"

What a sight! This is the history of the future. A great multitude (not just a few measly representatives), from every tribe, tongue and nation will be singing salvation's song.

Revelation 11:15
"Then the seventh angel sounded: And there were loud voices in heaven, saying, 'The kingdoms of this world have become the

kingdoms of our Lord and of His Christ, and He shall reign forever and ever!'"

Whoa! The future is looking bright! You're going to need sunglasses!

Revelation 19:1
"After these things I heard a loud voice of a great multitude in heaven, saying, 'Alleluia! Salvation and glory and honor and power belong to the Lord our God!'"

God's will has always been a great multitude in heaven! It looks like He gets His wish after all.

Revelation 5:9
"And they sang a new song, saying: 'You are worthy to take the scroll, and to open its seals; for You were slain, and have redeemed us to God by Your blood out of every tribe and tongue and people and nation…'"

Revelation 14:6
"Then I saw another angel flying in the midst of heaven, having the everlasting Gospel to preach to those who dwell on the earth - to every

nation, tribe, tongue, and people."

According to the book of Revelation, God's plan did not fail. The job got done. The Gospel was preached to every nation, tribe, tongue, and people.

Jesus said: Matthew 24:14
"And this Gospel of the kingdom will be preached in all the world as a witness to all the nations, and then the end will come."

> *According to the book of Revelation, somebody got the job done. Somebody rose up and made Jesus' last command their first priority.*

According to the book of Revelation, somebody got the job done. Somebody rose up and made Jesus' last command their *first priority*.

Somebody got in there and discovered God's will, gave money and their resources to it…and got the job done!

Who was it? Is it possible that it's written about you?

OUR FIRST PRIORITY

Somebody saw to it that this Gospel got delivered to every nation, tribe and tongue. Who was it?

Somewhere in the history of the future a church rose up and committed its best people and its best money to fulfilling the Great Commission. What church was it? Was it your church?

Somewhere a movement decided that it was its destiny to lead the world in harvesting the nations.

What movement was it? Was it your movement?

Somewhere, someone gave money, and lots of it, so the Gospel could be delivered. Who was it? Was it you?

You know, when you give your money to missions you are giving to the surest cause in the world. You are giving to a winner. You are investing in something for which the outcome has already been determined. Talk about insider trading! It would be illegal on Wall Street!

When you give to missions you are partnering with God in His plan for the ages. How cool is that!

According to the history of the future, the job got done. Some gave, some went, some prayed, some sent…but the job got done.

The prayer for laborers somehow got answered.

Luke 10:2
"Then He said to them, 'The harvest truly is great, but the laborers are few; therefore pray the Lord of the harvest to send out laborers into His harvest.'"

Is it possible that *you* are the answer to the prayer for harvesters?

Some time ago I was playing golf with my nephew on one of my visits from Australia to Arizona. We had just finished our game and we were waiting for our wives to come and pick us up. My nephew looked over and asked me a deep and probing question.

"Do you think the end of the world is near and do you believe the return of Christ is at hand?" I wanted to give him a real and honest answer and not just some glib rehearsed response. I said, "Well, I know I'm supposed to believe that. I've read the books that teach that, and I saw the movie, *A Thief In the Night* several times, which scared the daylights out of me. Everyone else I know seems to believe that. But I guess if I were to be real honest with you I'd have to tell you I've never really believed that His return is near, because Jesus said the Gospel had to first be preached in all the world as a witness to all nations. And I have never seen this mandate as the consuming passion of the Church. The consuming passion of the Church seems to be more about 'bless me' and 'help me' instead of 'consume me with Your cause'. So no, I've never really believed the end was near. But, in the past couple of decades something has happened that has changed my mind. The third world is sending out missionaries five times faster than we are, and whole nations are being saturated with the Gospel." I shared with him some of the amazing statistics of harvest and said that because of this I had changed my mind. "So even though I previously never believed His return was near, I certainly do now, as the Gospel spreads and multiplies throughout the earth. I believe time is shorter than ever and I believe that for the first time in the history of the world the finish line is in sight. Yes, Christ's return is imminent. But if I told you what I really believe, it would shock you."

Then I picked up my golf clubs and began to walk away. "Uncle Jack, wait a minute. What do you really believe?" I said, "I not only believe the return of Christ is at hand but I believe I am going to trigger the event!" He said, "Now you've got me scared!"

Come on friend, let's you and I trigger the greatest event in the history of the world – the return of the Lord Jesus Christ to this planet. If we get the Gospel to the lost, the least and the last, He will return. He's waiting on us.

> *God's plan will not fail. He's God. Is there anything too hard for Him?*

God's plan will not fail. He's God. Is there anything too hard for Him? His plan is to harvest the nations; to redeem the unreached, the unloved and the untold. This is God's prime directive.

Are you a part of His plan?

OUR FIRST PRIORITY

If not, why not?
Why not embrace the greatest destiny of all?
Why not embrace and invest in the plan of the ages?

Invest your life by going.
Invest your money by giving.
Invest your time by praying and serving.

I have inside information on this investment. It's a winner!

Matthew 19:29
"And everyone who has left houses or brothers or sisters or father or mother or wife or children or lands, for My name's sake, shall receive a hundredfold, and inherit eternal life."

'His sake' is all about nations, tribes and tongues receiving the Gospel. His sake is all about everyone being reached with the good news!
Has this good news reached you?
If it has, help us get it to the unreached.

About The Author

Well known for his ability to release finances for world harvest and stir a passion in Christians for the lost, Jack Hanes is the Senior Pastor of Penrith Christian Life Centre and President of the Australian Assemblies of God World Missions.

Raised in an unstable environment, Jack began his spiritual life at the age of 10 years and his ministerial life at 17, serving in the Southern Baptist Church as a pastor.

Jack was baptized in the Holy Spirit in 1971 while serving as a Southern Baptist Missionary in Alaska. He joined the U.S. Army Infantry in 1973 and was honorably discharged with commendations in 1976.

After his time in the US Armed Forces he moved back to his hometown, Yuma, Arizona, and joined Mt Zion Church, an independent charismatic church. He faithfully served 11 years there as Associate Pastor.

In August 1987, Mt Zion Church sent Jack and Carol and their family to pioneer a church in Australia. Subsequently, by September of that year, Mt Zion Christian Life Centre commenced in Penrith.

Nine years later, an exceptional event occurred. Two churches - Mt Zion Christian Life Centre and Penrith Christian Fellowship Centre – amalgamated as Penrith Christian Life Centre on 18 February 1996, with Jack Hanes accepting the role of Senior Pastor.

God has raised up Penrith Christian Life Centre to be on the cutting edge of a new dimension in missions, breaking new ground in the release of finances for world harvest and church planting. Penrith Christian Life Centre reaches into nations such as India, Indonesia, China, Far East Russia, North Korea and South Africa, while continuing to locally impact it's own city with Westcare Ministries and a new initiative called "*Making Life Better*" – a major city-wide outreach into the 50,000 homes of Penrith.

Jack, as President of Australian Assembly of God World Missions and Senior Pastor of Penrith Christian Life Centre, has a great vision to see churches become *First Priority* churches led by *First Priority* pastors (ie, making Jesus' last command to "*Go into all the world and make disciples*" their *First Priority*).

Jack's mainstay and number one fan is his wife Carol Hanes, who pastors Penrith Christian Life Centre alongside her husband. They have three children aged 22, 20 and 16.

Also Available By Jack Hanes

World Changers Network

"The World Changers Network is without a doubt the best pastoral resource I have ever seen… it has taken our church to a new level"
Ps Shane Cook, Newcastle Christian Outreach Centre

The World Changers Network will equip pastors and leaders in growing a missions dynamic in their church. The Network provides a 12 month module pack of Mission sermons complete with videos, audio tapes and sermon notes.

These resources will help create, develop, increase and intensify a missions passion, and help you raise money for your missions programs.

For more information:
PO Box 737 Kingswood
NSW 2747 AUSTRALIA
Phone (+61) 2 4736 3000
Fax (+61) 2 4736 2891
Email: pen.clc.mi@pnc.com.au
Website: www.worldchangersnetwork.com